Becoming Light in a Dark World

Martin Frankena

Copyright © 2013—Martin Frankena

All rights reserved. No part of this publication may be reproduced, stored in a retrieval system, or transmitted in any form or by any means, electronic, mechanical, photocopying or otherwise, without the prior written consent of the publisher. Short extracts may be used for review and teaching purposes.

The use of short quotations or occasional page copying for personal or group study is permitted and encouraged. Permission will be granted upon request.

Unless otherwise identified, Scripture quotations are from The New American Standard Bible, AMG Publishers, Chattanooga, TN 37422.

Other Scriptures versions quoted include:
English Standard Version, Modern King James Version, New English Translation, New International Version, New King James Version, New Living Translation, The Message, and the World English Bible.

ISBN 978-0-9890276-0-1

E-book ISBN 978-0-9890276-1-8

Cover Photo: Martin and Cindy Frankena

Back (insert photo): Glenn Landry

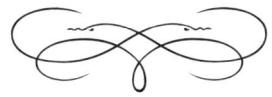

Acknowledgments

I am grateful to the Lord for the opportunity to work on this project and for the people who encouraged to finish the book and get it to print.

I am most thankful to my editor, Carol Miller, whose friendship, encouragement and commitment to clarity has been a great gift to me.

I am especially blessed by my wife, Cindy, who always believed in me more that I did.

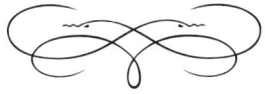

Preface

All books have a time of gestation and then the birth. This has been a long gestation, because it is not a simple subject. It has many valid sides, views and interpretations. This book in no way denies the validity of other views. My hope is to expand on one aspect of the subject to allow you to see in a deeper way the God given mandate on judgment and how it is to function in our daily lives.

The application of "not judging" can easily be misunderstood. This is not a command to disregard "sin," but to regard the "sinner" from God's point of view. It is also an admonition to us, to guard our hearts from turning against others who do not agree with us, hurt us or cause us or others harm - in other words, those who sin. The sinner is to be redeemed; the root of sin is to be destroyed.

Paul reminds us that we battle against an enemy we do not see; *For we wrestle not against flesh and blood, but against principalities, against powers, against the rulers of the darkness of this world, against spiritual wickedness in high places.*
Ephesians 6:12 KJV

Not seeing the enemy's hand, we often turn against one another, those we do see, those he uses as his instruments. When we do so, we give the enemy a way to create confusion, division and thus more harm. We must be alert and aware of his schemes that bring separation and ultimately destruction.

Anytime we act in ways that are unbecoming to God we open a door to sin.

Christ Jesus admonishes us: *"...if you are even angry with someone, you are subject to judgment! If you call someone an idiot, you are in danger of being brought before the court. And if you curse someone, you are in danger of the fires of hell."* Matthew 5:22 NLT

We are warned that any statement we make against a brother, or anyone else, is dangerous since it reveals a heart that is opposed to God.

Jesus came to save, not to judge. He came to manifest the love of the Father on earth for all. His desire truly is that no one should be lost.

There is also the other side of judging, with the admonition that we will and must judge, but I will leave that for a later time. For now I address Matthew 7:1-2. *"Do not judge, or you too will be judged. For in the same way you judge others, you will be judged, and with the measure you use, it will be measured to you."*

The issue (subject) of judging is far too large to address in one book, however, that is the case with all that God has given us. The deeper we delve into His word, the more there is to ponder. So I do not even begin to address the fullness of this topic, but I do write about that which He has given me. One of the difficulties with a book is the limitations in how much we can address, since the things of God continually grow the more we delve into them. There has to be a point where we say, "I must stop here."

With that in mind, I leave it unfinished, although there is so much more to be said on this subject.

Matthew 5: 43-44 *"You have heard that it was said, YOU SHALL LOVE YOUR NEIGHBOR and hate your enemy. But I say to you, love your enemies and pray for those who persecute you."*

If you can receive another point of view, another glimpse of His grace and mercy that will help keep you from falling in the trap of judgment, then the book has accomplished its purpose.

Table of Contents

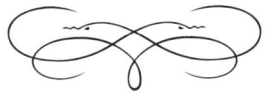

Acknowledgments		3
Preface		5
Introduction		11
Chapter 1	Call of the New Season: Becoming Light	15
Chapter 2	Clouding the Light	27
Chapter 3	Judgment: A Source of Darkness	37
Chapter 4	Learning Life	55
Chapter 5	Thinking God's Thoughts	63
Chapter 6	Judgment, Disagreement, and Confrontation	73
Chapter 7	God's Ownership and Makeover	91
Chapter 8	Living the New Life	111

Becoming Light

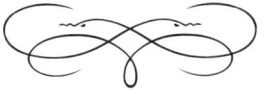

Introduction

"Do not judge, or you too will be judged. For in the same way you judge others, you will be judged, and with the measure you use, it will be measured to you." Matthew 7:1-2 NIV

It seems that even before we were able to speak or understand the world around us, we were coming to conclusions and making judgments.

Our personal likes and dislikes became the criteria for determining between good or bad, right or wrong. That which did not suit us was dismissed, devalued and when possible, removed. As we matured, our reactions became more ingrained. Having learned to prejudge people and events, we seldom consider whether the conclusions we draw are wrong or even just.

We learned to judge right from wrong, condemning not only the action but the person. Our judging was rarely about godly justice and the need for redemption. We thus created the adversarial culture we live in today, a culture of those who are "good" and accepted and those who are "bad" and rejected.

Now, as a born-again Christian, you come face to face with the mandate of the Kingdom of God which commands you to love your enemies, and do good to those who harm you—the very people you judged, rejected and isolated.

Our tendency is bent toward vengeance; we want the individual whose actions caused us pain to suffer in return and be isolated from our community. However, in the Kingdom you strive to redeem the person who caused the rift, loss, wound or defilement.

The belief that "They must be punished!" is not a Kingdom principle. In the Kingdom the perpetrator is given the opportunity to repent and turn from their error. Having done so, he is then able to make restitution (amends) for those things that caused the pain.

Vindictive, self-righteous judgment usually creates more anger, more separation and more pain. In the Kingdom however, the primary purpose is to call the sinner to repentance, reconciliation and restoration. "But you go and learn what this means: 'I desire mercy, and not sacrifice,' for I came not to call the righteous, but sinners to repentance." Matthew 9:13 In the Kingdom it is all about the sinner, their forgiveness and redemption. It is about finding the lost and restoring dignity and value to both the perpetrator and the one they hurt. "...in that while we were yet sinners, Christ died for us." Romans 5:8 This would make it seem that those who experienced the effects of the sinful actions must now invest part of their lives in the the life of the perpetrator.

Such is the Kingdom: the sinner is the focus of the cross and the reason for the shed blood. He must be redeemed, or at least given the opportunity to do so.

Harsh judgments label people and separate them from the very ones who are able to bring restoration and redemption; they fail to do the very thing Jesus died for. Godly judgment, which is meant to lead them to repentance, aims to bring revelation that sinful actions have painful consequences. Godly discipline is based on love, not retaliation. Although momentarily painful, it is ultimately restorative and life giving.

Yes, you are to judge, but the judgment is to bring revelation and restoration, to separate the sinner from the sin, to free him from the clutches of death and bring him to the fulness of life.

In Christ there is no condemnation. It is true that Jesus has already dealt with the eternal consequences of sin. However, we are still responsible for the damage caused by that sin. Judgment that brings only condemnation to an individual without initiating a restorative process, must be seen as counter productive. There is also no denying that there should be consequences to criminal activities, but judgment that is godly must be seen as a door to redemption.

It is important to be able to separate that which is a crime against God and humanity, from that which is a personal offense. A crime is always an offense and must be judged, but when you criminalize a personal offense, you move into self-righteous judgment, the very thing Jesus warns us about. However, it must nevertheless be confronted and forgiven.

"If therefore you are offering your gift at the altar, and there remember that your brother has anything against you, leave your gift there before the altar, and go your way. First be reconciled to your brother, and then come and offer your gift."
Matthew 5:23-24 WEB

A crime always violates the integrity of the community; an offense violates the integrity of the individual. Both need to be addressed. A crime affects the whole community, even those who are not aware of it. An offense on the other hand, is an interpretation of an action or an event that is a more personal, or intimate thing, usually between two people and must be dealt with accordingly.

Chapter 1

The Call of the New Season: Becoming Light

"Behold, I am making all things new." And He said, "Write, for these words are faithful and true."

Revelation 21:5

New Season

The Lord is asking, "Are you prepared for change?"

The standard answer to the Lord's question is, "Of course, I'm prepared, Lord. With You, I can do anything!" However, this answer is often based more in enthusiasm and the desire to impress Him than on deep conviction.

In this new season with God, we are going to face some major challenges to the way we live out our Christian life. With God you must always be prepared for change that challenges your inner structures and forces you to alter your response to the world around you.

As a member of the body of Christ, you are about to have your heart tested to reveal those things that anchor you to the world, those things that have no currency in heaven. Until you are tested, you really won't know the strength of your commitment to Christ as evidenced by the apostle Peter. *Peter said to him, "Even if all fall away, I will not."* Mark 14: 29 NET

To transition into the new, to change as He would have you change, you must be prepared to let go of the responses, beliefs, ideas and ideals — those things that have no real value in the realm that God is drawing you into. You must make room in your life for that which will sustain you and make you effective in the next phase of your walk with the Lord.

To be effective, to bear more fruit in keeping with the new season, pruning is necessary. *"I am the true vine, and My Father is the vinedresser. Every branch in Me that does not bear fruit, He takes away; and every branch that bears fruit, He prunes it so that it may bear more fruit."* John 15:1-2

As God prepares us for this new season, it becomes very evident that we do not have a clear sense of what it will look like or even what our function will be.

As I asked the Lord how this is going to happen, the only clue I received was in Proverbs 3:5-6. *" Trust in the LORD with all your heart And do not lean on your own understanding. In all your ways acknowledge Him, And He will make your paths straight."*

I am asked to trust. You are asked to trust.

Jesus came into the world as a light to men, to give direction, not understanding. *"The light shines in the darkness but the darkness has not understood it."* John 1:5 For the most part you want to understand the source of the light rather than just believe and follow the light. When you try to understand, you

| *The Call of the New Season: Becoming Light*

want to have some semblance of control. But Jesus did not come to be understood; He came to be believed and followed. God is declaring that you are not to "do," from a place of understanding, but from a place of faith. This is where the testing takes place—when your unknowing meets His knowing.

Becoming Light

Since my rebirth into the kingdom the Lord has asked me as a disciple to become "A Light to the World," to be noticeable in a unique way.

One of the Lord's objectives for our lives is to deal with our unwillingness to manifest His light and life in the world. He does this by confronting the way we (consciously or unconsciously) camouflage the evidence of His life to the immediate world we live in.

Most people don't mind being a light as long as it is confined to their faith community, which serves as a "bushel" that covers and protects them. *"...nor does anyone light a lamp and put it under a basket, but on the lampstand, and it gives light to all who are in the house."* Matthew 5:15 You can easily be a light in that hidden little place, where anyone who is under the bushel with you gets some of your light. However, in the world outside the bushel walls it is a different story. There we tend to hide, camouflaging our light from the world.

As long as you or I remain unnoticed in the world, we enable the enemy to use our hidden-ness to isolate us and neutralize our effectiveness. However, if you're going to be a light, you will be noticed. God wants to make you noticeable in a way that attracts the world to Him. As God transforms you in this new season, how others perceive and respond to you will change. Since change can cause tension, this will in all likelihood alter your relationship with others.

Becoming a Light Bearer

As Holy Spirit shines through you, be prepared for a greater level of transparency, something you may not be comfortable with or have experienced before. The light not only exposes your own areas of sin and brokenness, but will also do so in others. *"...and men loved the darkness rather than the Light, for their deeds were evil."* John 3:19 *"Now this is the gospel message we have heard from him and announce to you: God is light, and in him there is no darkness at all. If we say we have fellowship with him and yet keep on walking in the darkness, we are lying and not practicing the truth. But if we walk in the light as he himself is in the light, we have fellowship with one another and the blood of Jesus his Son cleanses us from all sin."* 1 John 1:5-7 NET

Christ-like integrity in you will raise a standard and change the atmosphere around you. The light of Christ always creates tension because it exposes darkness. When you become light, you will have an impact, either attracting people or driving them away. *"You are to be a light to the world." "Let your light shine before men in such a way that they may see your good works, and glorify your Father who is in heaven.* Matthew 5:14,16. The world is looking for that which is truly attractive and life giving, a source of truth which has light and life. In the prevailing darkness, you must become that light, giving direction and hope to those who are seeking the truth. *"But the path of the righteous is like the light of dawn, That shines brighter and brighter until the full day. The way of the wicked is like darkness; They do not know over what they stumble."* Proverbs 4:18-19

You are to become a unique manifestation of Christ, a carrier of light and life for others. As you mature into whom God intends you to be, you become a beacon that attracts others to the Christ in you. Your very actions become a reflection of His presence in you, a clear evidence of the Father. You cannot be hidden. This process of transformation is something we must cooperate with on a daily basis.

As you grow and mature you must ask yourself, "Is anyone finding enough light and life in me?" "Am I a true reflection of the work of Christ in me?"

As God transforms you into carriers of His light, He removes those things that do not reflect His character and nature, producing in you a sanctuary He can fill with Himself. He creates a place cleansed of any impurity so that His light can shine with greater and greater brilliance, transforming you from an obscure representation into a clear reflection of Jesus Christ. *"But we all, with unveiled face, beholding as in a mirror the glory of the Lord, are being transformed into the same image from glory to glory, just as from the Lord, the Spirit."* 2 Corinthians 3:18

Then Jesus again spoke to them, saying, *"I am the Light of the world; he who follows Me will not walk in the darkness, but will have the Light of life."* John 8:12

"...for you were formerly darkness, but now you are Light in the Lord; walk as children of Light (for the fruit of the Light consists in all goodness and righteousness and truth)," Ephesians 5:8-9

Ask yourself, "How bright is His light in me?" "Is the light of Christ in me attracting others?" When you interact with someone has something changed in them? Has some heaviness or some burden lifted? It is not always necessary to pray for people, but you need to be a prayer to them, a place of comfort, rest and restoration.

You carry the evidence - Do you show it?

St. Francis of Assisi once told his disciples. "Wherever you go, whatever you do, preach the gospel; and when absolutely necessary, use words." If you are not a reflection of the gospel, then what are you reflecting? The more the Word is living in and through you, the more attractive you become. People need to find Christ in you. The world is desperately looking for a true spiritual reality, something that will give meaning to their life. They are looking for that evidence in you which confirms your claim that Jesus changes lives by giving life. They are looking for evidence of the presence of God reflected in and through you. They are looking for someone to trust, someone in whom they can put their faith. Their demand for evidence compels they can put their faith. Their demand for evidence compels you to live a holy life, a life set apart not only from the world, but *for* the world.

Holy Spirit will teach you that which is on the heart of the Father. He wants you to reveal God's love and care for the world. *"For God so loved the world, that He gave His only begotten Son, that whoever believes in Him shall not perish, but have eternal life. "For God did not send the Son into the world to judge the world, but that the world might be saved through Him."* John 3:16-17

Jesus was (is) Light

A good question to ask yourself is, "Why did the people flock to Jesus?"

There was something in His Spirit that so touched them, that they would leave everything and follow Him for days, even into desolate places. True, healing and deliverance took place, but there was something else about Him that fed their spirit. He was a light in a dark world. *"In Him was life, and the life was the Light of men."* John 1:4

He gave them hope and direction to live a life that had purpose.

"The Light shines in the darkness, and the darkness did not comprehend it. There was the true Light which, coming into the world, enlightens every man." John 1:4-5, 9. Those who want truth and direction for their life will be drawn to wherever His Spirit is.

The question you must persistently ask yourself is, "Am I willing to be changed enough for that to happen?" It is not a question that is to be answered frivolously. You need to count the cost. When pressed, most people aren't really prepared to make the sacrifice.

> "If anyone comes to Me, and does not hate his own father and mother and wife and children and brothers and sisters, yes, and even his own life, he cannot be My disciple. Whoever does not carry his own cross and come after Me cannot be My disciple. For which one of you, when he wants to build a tower, does not first sit down and calculate the cost to see if he has enough to complete it? Otherwise, when he has laid a foundation and is not able to finish, all who observe it begin to ridicule him, saying, 'This man began to build and was not able to finish.'
> Luke 14:26-30

To come into this place in God requires a brutal examination of our values and the removal of everything that has no value in the Kingdom. Saying "Yes" to Him begins the process that exposes those areas of darkness in you that keep you from becoming life-giving to others. He confronts those hidden issues: the wounds of the past, the fears, the inadequacy and the shame. In His radiance you become aware of your own weaknesses and inadequacies; you may be tempted to shrink away rather than delight in and embrace the sanctification. Ask yourself, "What are those things in my life that I hold as totally not negotiable?" That have no kingdom value for my life?

Being Shaped by God

Knowing the truth does not mean that you will not resist it. You must allow the Word of God to shape your life. Most of us argue with God trying to reach a compromise. At the end of all our reasoning He will not change. He simply says, "That's the way it is. I am the Father, and your Father knows best!"

What was once acceptable isn't acceptable any more.

God is requiring a renewal at the core level of your being where all your beliefs and habitual thought patterns reside. He wants you transformed, but the old patterns resist change. Most people don't mind a little alteration, but they resist a change in life style. However, you were predestined and ordained to be conformed into the image of His Son, and what He has begun, He will finish. *"For I am confident of this very thing, that He who began a good work in you will perfect it until the day of Christ Jesus."* Philippians 1:6 NASB

The wonderful thing about this process is that God is gracious and extremely patient. *"For those whom He foreknew, He also predestined to become conformed to the image of His Son, so that He would be the firstborn among many brethren; and these whom He predestined, He also called; and these whom He called, He also justified; and these whom He justified, He also glorified.* Romans 8:29-30 *He predestined us to adoption as sons through Jesus Christ to Himself, according to the kind intention of His will, to the praise of the glory of His grace, which He freely bestowed on us in the Beloved."* Ephesians 1:5-6

That's His purpose. That's all He wants to do.

Maintaining the Old in the New Season

God is into drastic change! All change requires trust, and drastic change requires drastic trust. However, when you don't fully trust God's goodness, you will resist His transforming work in your life. Until the trust issue is settled, you want some say in the process and its outcome. That's where the conflict arises: He will not take your advice. He wants to do it His way. He *will* do it His way. You might as well comply.

When you said to Him, "I am yours," He took you at your word. However, when you consider the Lord a shareholder in your life, rather than a full owner, you still believe you that you have a say in how to live your life. You will resist changing the habitual ways of being and doing - particularly when you don't fully trust the one who is replacing the old patterns. You want to live by your own set of internal laws, laws you believe control your safety, well-being and comfort.

We are all creatures of habit who constantly resist and suspect those things that require a change in us. However, God declares, "I want you to operate in My Way."

Jesus declares, *"I am the way, and the truth, and the life; no one comes to the Father but through Me."* John 14:6 By receiving Him, the gateway to the Father, (John 10:9) you are changed; you become a new creation. You must now reflect that new creation to the world.

In Christ you have immunity from judgment.

> *"He who believes in Him is not judged; he who does not believe has been judged already, because he has not believed in the name of the only begotten Son of God. This is the judgment, that the Light has come into the world, and men loved the darkness rather than the Light, for their deeds were evil. For everyone who does evil hates the Light, and does not come to the Light for fear that his deeds will be exposed. But he who practices the truth comes to the Light, so that his deeds may be manifested as having been wrought in God."*
> John 3:18-21

Looking at the above passage, our tendency is to say, "Yes, Lord, they sure do love darkness," rather than "Lord, that's me as well, isn't it?" God's truth will challenge those beliefs which you accept as right and true. He may declare them to be bankrupt, of no value in the kingdom. He is after radical change.

Chapter 2

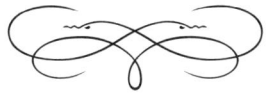

Clouding the Light

I asked the Lord one day, "How do I become a light? He impressed upon me:

> "Don't be an offense."

> "Don't take on an offense."

> "Don't judge an offense."

I understood that these are keys to live by in this season of change.

Don't be an Offense

The very life and light of God is released and becomes resident within you when you come to Christ. The light reveals darkness in you and the world. *"This is the judgment, that the Light has come into the world, and men loved the darkness rather than the Light, for their deeds were evil. For everyone who does evil hates the Light, and does not come to the Light for fear that his deeds will be exposed. But he who practices the truth comes to the Light, so that his deeds may be manifested as having been wrought in God."* John 3:19-21

Therefore it is important to walk in grace and the love of God, or you can easily create an offense in others. As a follower of Christ, you can't compromise with anything that does not bring glory to God, or you offend and disgrace the name you carry. As a Christian you must be an instrument of peace. However, who you are in Christ will cause an offense in the world. Jesus in you will always offend those who love darkness.

In your Christian walk, you will set up a standard that will challenge the standards of the world and more often than not cause an offense.

Offense Happens When You Don't Reflect Truth

When your relationship to the Lord is not real or apparent, you fail to image (reflect) Jesus and the Father. You cannot represent someone you do not know; if you try, you will only scandalize the very ones you allege to represent by portraying a lifeless and shallow caricature of the real, creating an offense in the eyes of the world.

Failing to Bring Hope

When you claim to bring hope and you don't reflect it in your life, you offend. Christian leaders, who do not model the life, hope and standard of the Christian walk, create an offense.

When your life reflects the nature of Jesus, you carry no judgment or condemnation of others. You love the sinner and will sacrifice your life to set him free from the sin. People ought to experience significance in your presence, not judgment. When they do, you open a door that allows them to embrace a new reality full of hope for a changed life.

The Careless Judgment

As you imitate Christ, you live out of the abundance of Holy Spirit, aware that all your words and actions have consequences.

Jesus makes a declaration to the effect that carelessness is a sin, for which you will be accountable on the Day of Judgment. *"But I tell you that every careless word that people speak, they shall give an accounting for it in the day of judgment. For by your words you will be justified, and by your words you will be condemned."* Matthew 12:36

Your words and actions must always guard the dignity and the integrity of others. It is far too easy to wound or offend when you are flippant, or too casual in your interactions. The careless word is often an unplanned or unguarded reaction that rises from and reveals the heart, finding expression through indignation, anger or sarcasm.

When you are careless, you become thoughtless to the point of being "sloppy" with your relationships. It means that you are not valuing, or you are taking the other person for granted. Both of these attitudes are signs of negligence in a relationship. It should therefore come as no surprise when others are offended or that there are negative consequences to your careless words or actions.

Jesus was never careless about anything. He only said what he heard the Father say and only did what he saw the Father doing. If you desire to be an imitator of Him, you can no longer be careless with your words or your actions. Carelessness wounds!

Your words and actions have the power to heal or to wound. The careless word is often self-serving and has no consideration for the effect or the consequences it may have. It must be rooted out with intentionality. Careful use of words shields others from the unnecessary wounds.

When you truly value who you are, you will not be careless with anything you say or do. The more you begin to recognize and accept the value God sees in you, and wants to show others through you, the more aware you become that your words are powerful. Using them carelessly is negligence on your part and wounding to others.

You may need help rooting out the carelessness from your life. This can best happen in a life giving relationship with God, other people and in community. *"All scripture is given by inspiration of God, and is profitable for doctrine, for reproof, for correction, for instruction in righteousness."* 2 Timothy 3:16 NKJV

Risking Offense

Bringing a corrective word or an observation about someone's behavior is confrontational and can be risky; there is always a possibility that they will be offended. Therefore, when you present truth that is meant to correct, it needs to be done with love and grace, with a regard for the other person's well being. This requires a new discipline of the mind, bringing it under the guidance of and submission to Holy Spirit. *"And do not be conformed to this world, but be transformed by the renewing of your mind, so that you may prove what the will of God is, that which is good and acceptable and perfect. For through the grace given to me I say to everyone among you not to think more highly of himself than he ought to think; but to think so as to have sound judgment, as God has allotted to each a measure of faith."* Romans 12:2-3

Bringing your thought life under discipline is not an easy task at the best of times, but absolutely necessary when you are confronted by an offense. *"For they disciplined us for a short time as seemed best to them, but He disciplines us for our good, so that we may share His holiness. All discipline for the moment seems not to be joyful, but sorrowful; yet to those who have been trained by it, afterwards it yields the peaceful fruit of righteousness."* Hebrews 12:10-11

All correction, any confrontation carries with it an element of risk. Occasionally, my wife will tell me that something I said or did was not very sensitive or maybe even hurtful. My response is usually, "You've got to be kidding! No, I didn't say that." "Yes, you did!" She will say, usually with a smile. When bringing correction to people, there is always a risk of consequences. It's a risk she willingly takes for my sake. Since I trust that she wants what is best for me, I want to make the changes needed so as not to offend in the future. I need her eyes to see my blind spots. You and I need people in our lives who will challenge our self perception, to help examine what we are doing or what is going on within us.

Confrontation is to save relationships (yours or someone else's), not to win the day.

Don't Carry an Offense

Offense Can Draw You into Legalism

When you are offended the tendency is to want some form of retribution. In the Old Testament Israel is told to "Love your friends, love your people, and hate your enemies." Jesus does not invalidate this command. He simply says, "Rise above it; in addition, love those who offend you." It runs against our nature to love those who offend; we are conditioned to think otherwise.

Jesus declares, Change your attitude. From now on you are to love your enemies, those who offend you; actually, you must love all people. If you want to shine, pray and intercede for those who hurt you. Luke 6:27, Matthew 5:44.

Unless you have the mind of Christ you will not grasp the depth or the significance and power behind that statement.

Offense and Bitterness

Without a change of heart, you live by rules that have no life in them. These rules are based on worldly standards that you learned to embrace to protect yourself as the result of hurts and unjust treatment, where the usual response is, "It's not fair!" "It is not right!" "I am going to get even."

The unresolved hurts and offenses breed resentment that lead to bitterness. *"Pursue peace with all men, and the sanctification without which no one will see the Lord. See to it that no one comes short of the grace of God; that no root of bitterness springing up causes trouble, and by it many be defiled."* Hebrews 12:14-15

Bitterness has an incredible ability to poison the heart and darken the light within you.

An Offense is Always an Offense

An offense, real or perceived, always creates a fracture in a relationship and a blockage to the flow of life in you.

Even a misunderstanding can still cause an offense. It really doesn't matter if the other person intended to offend or not; when you are offended, you are offended. Anger either motivates us to deal with an issue in a godly way, or is internalized or vented in a way that brings discord. To avoid possible conflict you must address and clarify the issue quickly, otherwise you open the door that allows bitterness to come into your life.

Understand that where there is judgment and condemnation, there is unforgiveness, which releases bitterness into your heart.

Don't Judge an Offense

The Cascading Effect of Judgment

Condemning judgments block the Lord's light in us. A received offense leads to judgment; judgment leads to condemnation and condemnation leads to bitterness, contaminating all those involved. Judgment creates a distorted view of the offender. Even those associated with the offender are tainted by the condemnation, in effect banishing them from part of your heart and separating them from your fellowship

Response to Offense

No matter how you think about it, taking on an offense is sin. Anytime you respond in anger or hurt feelings, or try to ignore it by internalizing the pain, you allow bitterness a foothold. A proper response is, "Lord, I forgive them. Lord, please forgive them." Then ask the Lord, "Why is this offending me?" "Is there something in me that needs to be changed?"

An offense is disempowered when you pray blessing on the one who hurt you. Until you can pray for them with some degree of fervor, you may still be holding some measure of bitterness. Ask Holy Spirit to identify those harmful judgments as they rise up in you. You may soon find that you have a much greater tendency to judge than you ever thought.

"Lord, I can't change unless you change me. Help me see things from Your perspective."

In your daily experiences—i.e., when somebody ignores you, cuts you off in traffic, or takes your parking spot—if your first response is, "Oh Lord bless them…" then you are in a good place. However, if you judge and label them "Inconsiderate, Rude, Stupid, etc.," your heart is closed and turned away, stopping you from blessing them. Any level of frustration, irritability and anger will increase if it is not laid at the foot of the cross. When you have these reactions, you may not even consider that this is darkening the very light within you, diminishing how people see you.

Being Dulled

A question to ask yourself is, "Am I reflecting Jesus enough to make Him attractive to those whose life I touch?" If not, what is clouding the light? Could it be that the offenses you are holding on to have blocked the light in you?

Chapter 3

Judgment: A Source of Darkness

Slavery of the Heart – Judging People Rather than Actions

Jesus reveals the heart of God in an account in John 8. Some Pharisees and Saducees come to him with a woman caught in the act of adultery. They declare that the law clearly states she is guilty and must die.

"What do you say?" they ask. In this violent and noisy scenario there is little compassion.

Seemingly unconcerned, he stoops down and writes in the dirt.

They are standing around Him demanding his decision. He, however, continues to write in the dirt. Believing they had trapped him, they wait. If Jesus agrees with them, he will lose favor with the people; if he disagrees, he is condoning sin and in open opposition to the law of God. They want to discredit Him. He wants to release them from their self-righteousness.

He knows that judgment that allows no room for redemption is merciless and leads away from the heart of God.

Using the law in their attempt to trap Jesus, they bring the woman to the only one who can save her. Jesus does not challenge the law, but he challenges their righteousness. *"Whichever one of you is without sin, carry out your judgment of her."* John 8:7 Author's paraphrase

By demanding true righteousness, Jesus asks them to examine their own hearts. When they do, from the eldest to the youngest they disqualify themselves. He challenges their hearts, not their interpretation of the law. In their zeal for the law, they stopped having compassion. *"He has shown you, O man, what is good. And what does Jehovah require of you but to do justice and to love mercy and to walk humbly with your God?"* Micah 6:8 MKJV

> *"Even in darkness light dawns for the upright, For the gracious and compassionate and righteous man."* Psalm 112:4 NIV

He says, "Any of you who is without sin go ahead and continue in your judgment; the rest of you may be excused." Jesus gives them a way out of their narrow, legalistic mindset.

To paraphrase it, "Yes, she has sinned, she has messed up. However, before you carry out your judgment, I will add this stipulation: only those of you who are truly righteous, without sin, are qualified to carry out the judgment."

Suddenly, there is an awareness that godly judgment requires a righteousness they did not have. They experienced something new, something they had not known before—a touch of grace and mercy.

Jesus is introducing the fulfillment of the law.

> *"Do not think that I came to abolish the Law or the Prophets; I did not come to abolish but to fulfill."* Matthew 5:17

> *"For of His fullness we have all received, and grace upon grace. For the Law was given through Moses; grace and truth were realized through Jesus Christ."* John 1:16-17

> *"For judgment will be merciless to one who has shown no mercy; mercy triumphs over judgment."* James 2:13

The Pharisees and Scribes planned to use this woman who broke the law to trap Jesus and destroy them both. Within the confrontation, both the woman and her accusers are set free.

This passage in John reveals God's heart: kindness, mercy and grace to all. He provides the accusers with an opportunity to rethink their actions and embrace mercy.

Her accusers are gone. There is no one left to condemn her, to carry out the judgment. He tells her, "Lady, you messed up." He doesn't sugar coat it. There is no judgment on His part, only an admonition. "Don't do this again."

Looking at the context, most of us would say that Jesus was

addressing the self righteousness of the Pharisees, and He was, but He was also releasing them from their blind slavery to the law by giving them a revelation and a taste of the heart of God.

He *loved* them. That's why He came.

The problem with the Pharisees was that they just couldn't hear Him because their hearts were in the wrong place. Their hearts were hardened; they judged from a perspective that didn't give life to anyone, including themselves.

Judging from a self-righteous position makes you an enemy; it separates and creates conflict. You must address sin to hold the person accountable, but do it without condemnation or rejection. This makes it easier for the person to take responsibility for their actions without becoming defensive. This is critical: don't judge to condemn. Do, however, insist on accountability.

Jesus knew that the woman had sinned, and broken the law, but He does not condemn her. He simply says to her, "You have offended. Don't do that anymore."

"Let him who is without sin…"

Jesus asks us every time we judge, "Are you without sin in this?" He is not accusing us, but he is reminding us that we have all sinned and are therefore in need of mercy and redemption. *"…for all have sinned and fall short of the glory of God,"* Romans 3:23. *"If we say that we have no sin, we are deceiving ourselves and the truth is not in us. If we confess our sins, He is faithful and righteous to forgive us our sins and to cleanse us from all unrighteousness. If we say that we have not sinned, we make Him a liar and His word is not in us."* 1 John 1:8-10

The sins of others must remind us of our own frailty and need for mercy. When you create your own righteousness, you are not only trying to avoid God's judgment, but are also denying your own need for mercy. Self-righteousness precludes mercy.

Judgment and Power

Judgment is always about the enforcement of rules. When you judge you decide what the rules are and how they should be kept.

Exercising judgment is always done from a real or perceived position of power and authority. Therefore when you judge you are often assuming the authority of God, trying to use His power to condemn or acquit someone without first examining your own heart or fully knowing all that has taken place.

When judging out of anger or fear, you can easily move into the place of vengeance or control, which moves you out of the will of God. Such a judgment usually involves some form of condemnation that leaves little room for mercy or the grace of God to bring redemption through you. This form of judgment is for the most part self-serving and sinful. It doesn't exclude you, or isolate you from God, but it dims your ability to be a light for others.

> *"For I am persuaded that neither death, nor life, nor angels, nor principalities, nor powers, nor things present, nor things to come, nor powers, nor height, nor depth, nor any other creature, shall be able to separate us from the love of God which is in Christ Jesus our Lord.* Romans 8:38-39 NKJV

Most of us believe we can judge with impunity anyone who does not agree with us. When you judge from a place of self-righteousness you judge from a sinful mindset that gives a feeling of control and therefore significance.

It's very hard to give up the judge's robe and the gavel when you don't have love or mercy for the one you accuse. When you judge to punish, you miss the heart of God. God disciplines those He loves.

Self Righteous Judgment

> *"And you have forgotten that word of encouragement that addresses you as sons: "My son, do not make light of the Lord's discipline, and do not lose heart when he rebukes you, because the Lord disciplines those he loves, and he punishes everyone he accepts as a son."* Hebrews 12:5-6 NIV

> *"Then it happened that as Jesus was reclining at the table in the house, behold, many tax collectors and sinners came and were dining with Jesus and His disciples. When the Pharisees saw this, they said to His disciples, "Why is your Teacher eating with the tax collectors and sinners?"* Matthew 9:10-11

"For John came neither eating nor drinking, and they say, 'He has a demon!' "The Son of Man came eating and drinking, and they say, 'Behold, a gluttonous man and a drunkard, a friend of tax collectors and sinners!' Yet wisdom is vindicated by her deeds." Matthew 11:18-19

The judgment of the Pharisees brought Jesus' integrity and godliness into question; He was eating with people they did not associate with because they truly believed that God was against those they considered sinners.

In other words, those people did not measure up to the Pharisee standard of righteousness; therefore, they were seen as sinners and unclean, not the kind of people a godly man would associate with, even less share a meal with. Their judgment was based on their assessment of His actions.

"How come He is hanging out with those people when He claims that He is so close to God?" That was a conflict that they could not understand. "How can He do this? Can't He see?" They had decided that they knew what was godly, and what wasn't, and Jesus did not measure up to their ideal of holiness. When Jesus hears this, He says, "You believe that you don't need Me because you claim to be righteous." *'It is not those who are healthy who need a physician, but those who are sick. But go and learn what this means: 'I desire compassion and not sacrifice,' I did not come to call the righteous, but sinners."* Matthew 9:12-13 NASB

Judgment that Blocks Prayer

Self-righteousness makes it particularly difficult to embrace the grace and mercy of the Lord, since you are deciding what is acceptable to God and what is not. Passing judgment on anyone makes it very difficult to pray for them. Your heart is not in it; your heart is still in a condemning posture.

Whenever you want to judge you need to defer to the Lord, asking Him, "Lord, how do You see them?" Once you have that revelation it is much easier to pray. It's the attitude of heart that is always the key concern.

Judgment of Comparison

When you compare, you judge. This becomes so much a part of your nature that you are not even aware of doing it. In the process you dim your impact in the world. Comparing yourself to others, either as better or less than, is a form of judgment that carries consequences which will affect you and your relationship with others.

> *"For in the way you judge, you will be judged; and by your standard of measure, it will be measured to you.* Matthew 7:2

> *"For through the grace given to me I say to everyone among you not to think more highly of himself than he ought to think; but to think so as to have sound judgment, as God has allotted to each a measure of faith."* Romans 12:3

> *"Therefore let us not judge one another anymore, but rather determine this—not to put an obstacle or a stumbling block in a brother's way."*
> Romans 14:13

God's Grace in Weakness

Most people fear having a weakness exposed. When it happens, they tend to withdraw, believing that somehow the exposure disqualifies them, rather than trusting that it is God's grace bringing to light what which otherwise keeps them in a place of darkness. That which you want to hide, God wants to expose. He wants to purify that area of your life and as long as you try to hide it, you won't reflect His glory.

You must recognize that when God exposes something in you it is to set you free from "it." It is to bring you into blessing, not punishment. However, when you expose something in someone it is usually to bring judgment. It is seldom done with a heart to raise them above their current position, but often to bring condemnation. *"My brethren, if any among you strays from the truth and one turns him back, let him know that he who turns a sinner from the error of his way will save his soul from death and will cover a multitude of sins."* James 5:19-20 Love covers a multitude of sins.

You can see an illustration of this in Scripture the night before Jesus dies. He is telling the disciples that they are about to abandon him, and Peter makes this heartfelt declaration, "You know, Lord, they might, but I won't!" He declares that his faithfulness and integrity are beyond anything the others have. He is implying, "Lord, I agree with you. Those guys haven't got what it takes. I have watched them for a while and they are really not as committed as some of us are."

> "But Peter said to Him, 'Even though all may fall away because of You, I will never fall away.'" Jesus said to him, 'Truly I say to you that this very night, before a rooster crows, you will deny Me three times.' Peter said to Him, 'Even if I have to die with You, I will not deny You.' All the disciples said the same thing too." Matthew 26:33-35

Peter had a special relationship with Jesus.

"You are Peter and on this rock…"

Peter held a special place with Jesus.

Peter had revelation from the Father, "You are the Christ…"

Peter trusted Jesus; he walked on water when Jesus told him to.

He was one of the first apostles chosen by the Lord.

He was self-reliant. However, his self-reliance was his weakness.

Because of this, Jesus needs to show Peter this area of weakness that he is blinded to: "Peter, I need you to realize that what you're doing is dangerous. I understand your sense of loyalty and your belief that they might run, and that you believe that you are never going to leave me. I want you to understand there is a weakness in you that must be exposed. So, Peter, not only are they going to leave, but you are going to deny me three times, and it is going to happen in a specific way and time."

There is no judgment or condemnation in The Lord's statement. This is just a fact—something the Lord knows is going to happen.

When it happens, Peter recognizes his unimaginable weakness, his incredible short fall, and he weeps. Not only has he betrayed his mentor, his friend and Lord, but at that moment he recognized that he isn't who he thought he was.

The reality is that Jesus had already told him not only about his denial, but also about his healing. *"...By the way, Peter, when you are restored, go back and help the others. However, right now you need to have a revelation about the true depth of your loyalty and what you think is your strength, and once you come to terms with the fact that you are not as strong or better than the rest or as loyal as you think, you will be healed and restored."*
1 Corinthians 15:4-5 Author's paraphrase

When God restores, something amazing happens.

Peter experiences a remarkable change. He had truly believed that he would not fail, yet he fell short of what he believed about himself. Until he was tested he did not know what the Lord knew about him. Once Peter became aware of his limitations, God could teach him and change him. When you are restored, expect a change, and not only for yourself, but also for others.

How often do you make a judgment about a person or a situation without even being fully aware of doing it? Whenever you think or say, "I am better than they are." "That is stupid." "How could they?" you are making a judgment. God will say to you, "Watch it!" because you don't know or understand what changes the Lord is making in the background. When you judge, you often have not thought about the consequences of what you are doing.

We have never fully understood the impact of our judgments. The example of Peter is wonderful!

Whenever I notice or hear about someone doing something wrong, my tendency is to make a judgment and then ask God to carry out the sentence. However, the Lord is clear when He says that is not the way to live. *"But I say to you who hear, love your enemies, do good to those who hate you, bless those who curse you, pray for those who mistreat you."* Luke 6:27-28

The moment you judge someone who has failed, you give the enemy a right to release bitterness into your heart that will quickly separate you from the person and bring defilement into the relationship.

If Judgment Gives You Pleasure, You Have Missed God.

When you want to judge you are out of the will of God. He says, "No, you mustn't do this." "That's not My heart. Something needs to change in you."

> *"Do I have any pleasure in the death of the wicked,"* declares the Lord God, *"rather than that he should turn from his ways and live?" For I have no pleasure in the death of anyone who dies,"* Declares the Lord God. *"Therefore, repent and live."*
> Ezekiel 18:23,32

> *"Bless those who persecute you; bless and do not curse."* Romans 12:14

> *"Pursue peace with all men, and the sanctification without which no one will see the Lord. See to it that no one comes short of the grace of God; that no root of bitterness springing up causes trouble, and by it many be defiled;"* Hebrews 12:14-15

People will offend you. When they do, ask the Lord what it is about them that He loves so much."

You must always be aware of what Jesus warned us about: If you judge someone or condemn someone, you are opening yourself up to a similar consequence.

Prejudices: Learned Judgments Based on Experience and Expectations

If you are asked for your first impression of words, such as a "politician" or "used car salesman," or "an illegal," the typical response is usually negative. This is a judgment.

It is common to have created labels for certain people, and these labels carry a prejudgment about what they are and what they do. These judgments resurface the moment you meet a person or a situation that reminds you of the original event you judged.

Instantly the prejudgment is there.

It is necessary to break these habitual ways of thinking and reacting. It's not just the deliberate judgments you make, it's the unconscious predispositions you carry which are so damaging. These are the prejudices you carry into your daily life, which will determine how you respond to a diversity of people and situations. Prejudices (instantaneous and predetermined judgments) mean that you don't have to go through the process of assessing each person or situation you meet, since you have already prejudged it.

These are the beliefs and determinations you learned through your parents, teachers, friends and culture. You absorbed their expectations about races, ages, gender, nations, professions, sports teams, religions, etc...

Ask the Lord, "What is my greatest prejudice? Show me, and teach me how to come in the opposite spirit."

These prejudices can also be based on experiences that led to conclusions and beliefs that are now used as a standard to decide between Acceptable and Unacceptable, right and wrong, and who to trust and mistrust. These conclusions may have nothing or very little to do with the present situation.

I grew up in an age when a person's color determined his place in society, gender was more important than ability and everyone from Russia was considered an enemy. Those were the accepted prejudices and we never gave them a second thought or even considered those beliefs to be unjust. Prejudice creates judgments which are our preconceived notions of righteousness. They create separation and enmity, releasing anger, bitterness and suspicion in our heart.

Your prejudices control you, and usually alienate and hurt rather than correct, bless and heal.

Self-Judgment: Proclaiming Disqualification

"I know how to get along with humble means, and I also know how to live in prosperity; in any and every circumstance I have learned the secret of being filled and going hungry, both of having abundance and suffering need. I can do all things through Him who strengthens me."
Philippians 4:12-13

"And looking at them Jesus said to them, "With people this is impossible, but with God all things are possible." Matthew 19:26

You can even have prejudices against yourself, which are just as painful and alienating as those you hold against others.

What you say or think about yourself can diminish you. Your judgments about yourself obscure and block the light of God in you. You may believe that your self-judgments are good and righteous: "I'm just being humble." However, what you call humble is often pride masquerading as humility; it is false humility, and it is sinful. Godly humility speaks the truth and accepts the truth. It doesn't exaggerate it or diminish who you are in God or His gifts in you.

Self-condemnation

Self condemnation is the result of judging oneself, of taking the judgment seat on behalf of God. Holy Spirit convicts us of sin to bring change, to release blessing and not condemnation. However, rather than seeking and receiving God's forgiveness, we judge and condemn ourselves. Using our own set of rules, we determine what we must do to atone for our failure.

We may say "I know that God has forgiven me," but as far as we are concerned, it is not enough. We feel that we still need to suffer and make up to God for that which He's already declared as "Forgiven and forgotten."

We are often harder on ourselves than God is, and much less gracious. He forgives and chooses to forget; we on the other hand reluctantly grant ourselves a parole, certainly not a pardon. In this way we still carry a "record" of our faults that we can hold against ourselves at any time. We become our own worst enemy, relentlessly hounding ourselves for past mistakes, never forgetting or fully forgiving. Rather than accepting God's declaration of love, acceptance and forgiveness, we struggle to trust and believe God's mercy and grace toward us. We are much more comfortable degrading and devaluing ourselves.

The Lord wants to draw you to a place where you can say, "Lord, because of you I am blessed and therefore I'm a blessing! Today, even if I don't say a word, I expect to touch Your people with Your goodness." With that attitude your life will have an impact on others.

I am not saying that you are better than anybody else, but that you have something in you that is so life-giving that it radiates out of you. You may not always feel like it, you may not even act like it, but His presence in you makes it so nonetheless.

Taking On What Is Not Ours To Carry

Believing that as a member of the Kingdom, you must be able to do everything well, is a trap of the enemy. Your gifts are unique and serve a specific purpose in the plans of God.

> *"Now these are the gifts Christ gave to the church: the apostles, the prophets, the evangelists, the pastors and teachers. Their responsibility is to equip God's people to do his work and build up the church, the body of Christ.* Ephesians 4:11-12 NLT

When you believe that you must be able to do all things well, you are trapped in a cycle of failure, disappointment and self condemnation.

I once believed that if I did not lead people to the Lord I was failing God, and as a result someone was going to spend eternity in hell. I felt guilt ridden, a failure in my own eyes, and a disappointment to God.

I have since come to the realization that my gifting is to explore the Word, to teach and minister. That's enough; He will see to it that I will never get bored. However, as long as I believed that I needed to be able to do all things well I was doomed to fail and as a result I judged myself as inadequate and disqualified. I needed to break the cycle that led to self condemnation and disqualification, that kept me locked in a place of sinful judgment.

The turnaround came when I asked the Lord about my sense of failure and wondered how He felt about my lack of enthusiasm for what I believed were Kingdom mandates. His response was very liberating.

He said, "Unless you intend to replace Me, you're not going to do it. Be content with what I have given you."

That settled it.

Chapter 4

Learning Life

How does someone become so filled with negative judgments and opinions about themselves and others?

God's Standards versus Your Beliefs

The negative patterns modeled in the home and learned through life experiences become the blueprint on which most of your life is based. When these beliefs and patterns do not agree with Kingdom truth, you come into a conflict—you must either reject Godly direction, believing that you know better, or willingly submit to the Lord, letting go of your ungodly self-protective patterns of thinking and behavior.

These ungodly patterns are deeply ingrained; they are the familiar responses, the road maps you follow without thinking. They are most often based on worldly values and your expectations of life. Where these ingrained patterns are not godly, they must be discarded and replaced with a new God-given way of thinking. Establishing these new thought patterns helps bring you into fullness of life.

> *"I call heaven and earth to witness against you today, that I have set before you life and death, the blessing and the curse. So choose life in order that you may live, you and your descendants, by loving the LORD your God, by obeying His voice, and by holding fast to Him; for this is your life and the length of your days, that you may live in the land which the LORD swore to your fathers, to Abraham, Isaac, and Jacob, to give them."*
>
> Deuteronomy 30:19-20

Choices

Almost all of your decisions are based on your beliefs and value judgments—established by the confidence and value you placed on certain people or things in your life. Most of these values and beliefs were established early in life by the decisions you made or were made for you by others—people of influence: parents, teachers, coaches, pastors, friends, the many voices that influenced your choices.

Often the criteria for your decisions were based on the foregone conclusions you came to as a result of what you were taught or experienced. When these negative conclusions became ingrained, they turned into prejudices, the unconscious judgments that formed a major part of your core belief system. As far as you were concerned they were the truth and therefore totally trustworthy.

Created and then Made

Years ago we got a dog. I never had to teach him to be a dog. I never had to teach him how to bark, what to do when he came to a tree or fire hydrant. He just knew.

We on the other hand are different. I came into this world as a clean slate. Because God created me with a mind that was waiting to be filled, my parents and significant others in my community had to teach me what I needed to survive and grow into a healthy, life giving, human being.

To the best of their ability, they began to deposit in me those things they believed I needed to survive in the world; some of what they taught me was good and some was not. However, as a child I could not tell the difference; as far as I was concerned it was all good and true.

Learning Values, Learning Life

Through their teaching and modeling I developed a whole system of values and beliefs that I carried with me into the world—the life tools they thought would keep me safe, out of harm's way. However, like most parents, they left some of the key life lessons unfinished, or for me to complete.

I saw my father as the wisest and most powerful man in the world. Whatever he said had to be true. I could not imagine him not knowing something, or worse, lying about it. My parents were my anchor, the safe harbor in the world I was becoming a part of. They were my source of life and therefore, as far as I was concerned, totally dependable and trustworthy. If that was true of them, it must also be true of others. I eventually learned through teaching and experience that people could not always be trusted.

My father taught me many things, but because of his own insecurities he failed to teach me or reflect the value of who I was and who he was in the sight of God. He lived in the tension of not knowing the love of God and therefore worked hard trying to prove his worth. As a result I also learned that what I did was worth more than who I was.

His lack of self confidence became one of his legacies to me.

He taught me that true value was not in who I was, but in what I did and how much I could earn.

He taught me how to be a husband, by his behavior and attitudes towards my mother.

He taught me how to be a man by the way he interacted with other men and women.

He taught me how to be a father by the way he disciplined me and gave value to the things I did.

He taught me how to be critical of what I did, always looking for the things that were wrong.

He taught me to work hard.

He taught me that my word should be my bond, enough to settle a matter.

He taught me about God by the way he prayed.

However, I was never taught one of the key things I needed for a full healthy life: the incredible love God has for me.

I never learned or heard:

> "This is who God is and how God loves you."
>
> "This is what He did for you at the cross."
>
> "This is how He gently deals with you when you fail."

What I did learn was that with God and man failure was unacceptable; works were the way to heaven, and when we suffered, it was a punishment for failure. These teachings kept me fearful and away from a God I thought was unapproachable. I judged Him as vindictive, distant and unpredictable. I quickly decided that the safest thing to do was to keep my distance from him.

I inherited my father's prejudices and attitudes that were based on fear. As a result I learned to withdraw and become fearful.

I learned that risking was dangerous and only done when there was no other option.

I quickly learned to judge people and be careful about whom I would allow into my life.

Those are some of the familiar prejudices, the family rules, that I was taught to keep me safe. I used them most of my life. These became the unconscious patterns that governed my life, the programs that ran in the background. I didn't have to think about them; they operated automatically, maintaining the patterns established from the time of my birth. I used those patterns and beliefs to stay safe and judge the world around me.

God now wants to change all of that.

You Imitate What You Value

Your thoughts and your actions are always a reflection of the significant people or influences in your life. You will imitate the people whose ideals and lifestyle you admire. Everyone tends to emulate and reflect an aspect of those who had or have a significant influence in his or her life.

You emulate that which you admire—good or bad.

Your life is a reflection of other people's influence in your lives—positive or negative.

My father had a tremendous influence on my life, because when I was a child he represented what I believed I should be like.

So I became a man in the fashion of my father.

I became a father in the fashion of my father.

I became a husband in the fashion of my father.

I judged and condemned in the fashion of my father.

It wasn't all bad, but it wasn't all good either.

You Live What You Judge

That which you have judged with condemnation carries with it a poison of bitterness you must release to the Lord, otherwise you will live through the thing you judged. It is a spiritual principle. *"For in the way you judge, you will be judged; and by your standard of measure, it will be measured to you."* Matthew 7:2

The ungodly judgment pattern in my life requires God's intervention, my repentance and correction, a letting go of the old patterns that brought no life or joy.

Today, I am thankful to my earthly father and my heavenly Father for all they brought into my life and the lessons I learned and continue to learn from both.

Chapter 5

Thinking God's Thoughts

There is a big difference between Godly Judgment and Sinful Judgment.

True Judgment

There is a form of judgment for which we are responsible: that is the judgment which distinguishes right from wrong.

Godly judgment focuses on the redemptive solution rather than condemnation for the individual. You can easily become snared into the ungodly when you allow your need for vengeance (rage, hatred, unforgiveness, bitterness, superiority) to enter your heart. This is the destructive and sinful part of judgment.

Adversarial Judgment versus Redeeming Judgment

Always try to look at people from God's perspective. God's judgment always has a redemptive side to it. His intention is and will always be to save, not to condemn. *"Do not judge according to appearance, but judge with righteous judgment."* John 7:24

Jesus did not come to judge the world, but to save the world. John 3:17. Nonetheless He will judge the hearts of men according to their own judgments, Matthew 7:1-2, Luke 6:37. Ultimately you choose how you will live now and in eternity. *"Therefore you have no excuse, everyone of you who passes judgment, for in that which you judge another, you condemn yourself; for you who judge practice the same things. And we know that the judgment of God rightly falls upon those who practice such things. But do you suppose this, O man, when you pass judgment on those who practice such things and do the same yourself, that you will escape the judgment of God? Or do you think lightly of the riches of His kindness and tolerance and patience, not knowing that the kindness of God leads you to repentance?"* Romans 2:1-4

> *"Do not speak against one another, brethren. He who speaks against a brother or judges his brother, speaks against the law and judges the law; but if you judge the law, you are not a doer of the law but a judge of it. There is only one Lawgiver and Judge, the One who is able to save and to destroy; but who are you who judge your neighbor? "*
> James 4:11-12

If someone runs a red light, you can say, "They ran a red light." That is a valid observation. However, if you say, "That stupid **&##* ran a red light" you have just made a condemning judgment presupposing that you are right or better than they are, which puts you in an adversarial posture and keeps you from praying the heart of God for that person.

> "But I say to you who hear, love your enemies, do good to those who hate you, bless those who curse you, pray for those who mistreat you.
> Luke 6:27-28

Adversarial, or Antagonistic Judgment

The most familiar judgment is adversarial or antagonistic: "Me against you," "Us against them."

This form of Judgment is (usually) meant to accuse and bring condemnation on the "other person," to make them accountable to you and your beliefs, which may not necessarily reflect God's way. It is often openly condemning, declaring the other person to be wrong, at fault, and out of God's will. Another form of judgment may come as an insinuation, hinting that the person has done something wrong or failed to do that which is right, often leaving them feeling confused, rejected, and isolated.

Adversarial judgment comes with disapproval and leads to separation. This is often followed by a period of probation where the other person has to prove himself again, with no guarantee of acceptance in the future. It leaves them lessened, devalued and separated from the very thing they needs for restoration: their community.

Redeeming Judgment

Redeeming judgment on the other hand has the future well being of the person in mind. It is meant to bring the heart of God into a difficult situation. Godly judgment keeps someone from knowingly or unknowingly remaining in or entering into a sinful situation that could harm them spiritually, emotionally, mentally or physically.

Redeeming judgment is meant to bring a positive change into the damaged relationship through restorative discipline, not punishment, and it always comes wrapped in grace and truth. Once the sin issue has been addressed, the person can now, hopefully, see their responsibility and embrace it, knowing that they are pardoned and accepted without ever having lost their value or significance.

Correction and restitution now becomes a natural step in restoration. Discipline is now seen as a benefit rather than punishment, not only to the offender, but also to the community in which they live.

Law and Legalism

Redeeming judgment with its correction and restitution does not excuse the breaking of laws or in any way allow you to ignore the law, whether they are the laws of God, or those of the land that are based on godly principles.

The law is still the law, and it must be kept; it is God's standard for wholeness and righteousness. Whatever the law directs has to be honored, not only in action but also in the heart. It is the attitude of your heart regarding this issue that you must contend with. That is always the crucial concern.

If someone steals something from you, you are not going to disregard it, saying "That's all right, I forgive them." You need to forgive, but you can't ignore the act. That would not benefit anyone, since you would be condoning sin and enabling someone's sinful behavior. They need to face the consequences of their actions, but they do not need to face your unforgiveness or revenge.

Law and Judgment

The law, and the consequence of breaking it, was never cancelled. It is still in effect today because the word of God does not change. There always is a response when the law is broken. The law is of no consequence until there is a judgment.

> *"Do not think that I came to abolish the Law or the Prophets; I did not come to abolish but to fulfill."* Matthew 5:17

The problem arises when you use the law to turn your hearts away from the one who failed. Again, it bears repeating, never condone the sinful action, or indicate that there are no consequences for these actions, but look at the heart of God for the one who failed.

Law and the Heart of God

When the law is no longer a vehicle that reveals your need for mercy and compassion, when it no longer offers a way to redemption, it has been turned into a system that offers little hope or opportunity for change. If the law becomes rigid and devoid of its intended life giving function, it no longer reveals the heart of God.

Jesus came to fulfill the law; He placed a capstone on it by declaring that God is love. Anything that does not have its foundation in that truth is not of Him.

When the law does not reveal the heart of God, you are lost in a place of isolation, fear and hopelessness.

Jesus came along and said, "By the way, I'm not going to abolish the law. I have come to fulfill the law by capping it with the love, grace and mercy of the Father. All that the law requires, I will deal with; it doesn't get cancelled. I will pay the whole price. All you need to do is accept my words, acknowledging that you have need of the Father's love and mercy. "

Judge Sin not the Sinner

Sin must always be judged. However, if you judge the one who offended you, you are in danger.

> *"But I say to you that everyone who is angry with his brother shall be guilty before the court; and whoever says to his brother, 'You good-for-nothing,' shall be guilty before the supreme court; and whoever says, 'You fool,' shall be guilty enough to go into the fiery hell. Therefore if you are presenting your offering at the altar, and there remember that your brother has something against you, leave your offering there before the altar and*

go; first be reconciled to your brother, and then come and present your offering. Matthew 5:22-24

You don't judge the apple of God's eye even though they are doing something you may not agree with or that you know is wrong. You are called to judge the action, to make others aware of the peril of their digression.

"If your brother sins, go and show him his fault in private; if he listens to you, you have won your brother. But if he does not listen to you, take one or two more with you, so that BY THE MOUTH OF TWO OR THREE WITNESSES EVERY FACT MAY BE CONFIRMED. If he refuses to listen to them, tell it to the church; and if he refuses to listen even to the church, let him be to you as a Gentile and a tax collector. Matthew 18:15-17

My brethren, if any among you strays from the truth and one turns him back, let him know that he who turns a sinner from the error of his way will save his soul from death and will cover a multitude of sins. James 5:19-20

"But you, why do you judge your brother? Or you again, why do you regard your brother with contempt? For we will all stand before the judgment seat of God." Romans 14:10

"Therefore let us not judge one another anymore, but rather determine this--not to put an

obstacle or a stumbling block in a brother's way."
Romans 14:13

"Do not speak against one another, brethren. He who speaks against a brother or judges his brother, speaks against the law and judges the law; but if you judge the law, you are not a doer of the law but a judge of it. There is only one Lawgiver and Judge, the One who is able to save and to destroy; but who are you who judge your neighbor?" James 4:11-12

Judgment can easily become a stumbling block, since your judgment creates a wall between you and the one you judge. Yes, you must always address the sin issue. However, the problem is that you often lump the sin and the sinner together. The gospel of Matthew has a good illustration of judgment. Jesus was eating with publicans and sinners.

"When the Pharisees saw this, they said to His disciples, 'Why is your Teacher eating with the tax collectors and sinners?' But when Jesus heard this, He said, 'It is not those who are healthy who need a physician, but those who are sick. But go and learn what this means: I DESIRE COMPASSION, AND NOT SACRIFICE, for I did not come to call the righteous, but sinners.'" Matthew 9:11-13

When Your Judgment Excludes God

There are times when you can be so sure of your conclusions about a situation that you don't even ask for God's guidance before judging, because you believe you know "His standards."

This was the problem the Pharisees struggled with in their relationship to Jesus. He is saying to them, "Don't decide who is acceptable to God and who is not – don't take the law into your own hands. In fact, when someone wrongs you, don't even claim that you have a right to demand judgment. Leave that to God."

Chapter 6

Judgment, Disagreement and Confrontation
Disagreeing versus Judgment

There is an enormous difference between disagreeing with someone and judging them. Disagreement is never a judgment unless it leads to some form of condemnation. Condemnation, however, is always the outworking of a judgment.

You *judge* when you condemn others for their views or actions that do not agree with your opinion.

When you *disagree*, you face your differences with the confident expectation that during the discussion you may discover a solution that not only delights you, but reveals the heart of God in the process. However, when you disagree and the ensuing discussion turns into an argument, the issue now becomes one of control where one wins and one loses. One dominates and the other must submit. This will inevitably create an ungodly response and a sinful conclusion.

You must confront when you disagree with someone or something that is in conflict with the word of God. The confrontation should be to address and resolve your differences on the issue; it must not be to attack the person. You can disagree with someone without dishonoring or judging them.

The Gift of Confrontation

Confrontation, which is often seen as conflict, and therefore avoided, is in reality a very vital gift from God that has remarkable life-giving possibilities.

> *"He whose ear listens to the life-giving reproof will dwell among the wise. He who neglects discipline despises himself, But he who listens to reproof acquires understanding. The fear of the LORD is the instruction for wisdom, And before honor comes humility."* Proverbs 15:31-33

Confrontation has two possible outcomes, and both reveal the heart. One brings satisfaction and produces growth; the other breeds resentment and creates division. One looks for solutions, the other for control. Most people, however, believe and expect a confrontation to be the equivalent of coming to verbal "blows," and in extreme cases, even physical ones.

> *"He who corrects a scoffer gets dishonor for himself, And he who reproves a wicked man gets insults for himself. Do not reprove a scoffer, or he will hate you, Reprove a wise man and he will love you. Give instruction to a wise man and he will be still wiser, Teach a righteous man and he will increase his learning."* Proverbs 9:7-9

When you approach an issue with a firm belief that the other person is wrong, you have already come with a condemning judgment (closed mind) which does not allow room for God's leading. You must recognize that your disagreement may simply mean that you have not yet acquired God's wisdom in a situation—that there is a solution which you haven't explored.

If you have misunderstood someone or a situation, or you don't have a right perspective on what is happening, you need to be able to discuss it to reach an understanding. It must be addressed and hopefully resolved to avoid confusion or ill feelings. In a godly confrontation, you are seeking a solution to something that has become a problem to one or both of you. You are committed to come to a resolution that honors both parties. Confrontation, when done with that in mind, brings clarity to a situation by helping resolve differences in a godly way, which in turn, facilitates course corrections in your life or the lives of others.

Fear: a Blockage to Godly Resolution

Many people won't confront because they fear that it will create a conflict. This fear of confrontation is in reality a fear of man. You may justify your unwillingness to confront by stating that you don't want to offend, hurt or alienate, but that usually is an excuse to mask the fear.

Submitting to pressure or fear places you into a position that can easily cause you to compromise with someone or something you know to be wrong. You must see confrontation as a God given tool to resolve a conflict and avoid a condemning judgment. Confrontation when done properly creates a pathway for resolution and mutual growth.

Consequences of Not Confronting

Faulty conclusions about a person or a situation will most likely create a negative judgment. This is the reason to confront an issue: to ask the other person(s) for clarification, or to state your position on an issue, to make sure there is no misunderstanding. The goal is to resolve the differences without judgment, condemnation, or accusation of any kind. This does not mean you have to agree on all things, but you should have an understanding where the other person stands on an issue. It does not mean that you condone sin, but that you seek the heart of God for the person and the situation. Failure to confront, to clarify the situation, may well cause you to make a decision based on wrong impressions, biases, or incomplete information. Making decisions based on incorrect information can easily lead to ungodly judgments.

These judgments release condemnation and create a stumbling block between you and the other person.

The Way of Confrontation

As with judgment, you can approach confrontation from two perspectives: adversarial or redemptive.

One of the main problems with confronting is that it is usually done from an adversarial point of view. Approaching it with a redemptive perspective, you try to correct a wrong, clarify a perceived wrong, or stop a potential wrong. The confrontation must be seen as a win/win situation for you and a lose/lose condition for the enemy. When you approach confrontation from an adversarial position, you fail to see that there is a higher purpose—to restore or protect relationships.

Since most people are not familiar with the language of disagreement, the dynamics or purposes of godly confrontation have not been explored. As a result you approach confrontation, not with redemptive purpose, but with the need to "Win." At other times, you avoid it all together because you are fearful or feel inadequate to the task.

Confrontation is meant to produce an attitude of cooperation by strengthening a relationship, yet most often it is seen as threat and therefore an offense to be avoided.

Jesus Model

Jesus confronted all the time and He wasn't being heartless about it. When He confronted, He was simply saying, "This situation, or this attitude, needs to change."

He confronted a woman who had been caught in adultery.

He confronted a woman at the well.

Both women left feeling more alive and enlightened than before He met them.

> *"So the woman left her waterpot, and went into the city and said to the men, 'Come, see a man who told me all the things that I have done; this is not the Christ, is it?' They went out of the city, and were coming to Him."* John 4:28-30

In the house of Simon the leper, Jesus again confronts both Simon and the disciples.

> *"Now when Jesus was in Bethany, at the home of Simon the leper, a woman came to Him with an alabaster vial of very costly perfume, and she poured it on His head as He reclined at the table. But the disciples were indignant when they saw this, and said, "Why this waste? "For this perfume might have been sold for a high price and the money given to the poor. But Jesus, aware of this, said to them, "Why do you bother the woman? For she has done a good deed to Me. "For you always have the poor with you; but you do not always have Me. "For when she poured this perfume on My body, she did it to prepare Me for burial. "Truly I say to you, wherever this gospel is preached in the whole world, what this woman has done will also be spoken of in memory of her."* Matthew 26:6-13

They needed to recognize their prejudices, to become aware that their attitudes were in conflict with Jesus' heart. Their conclusion about the woman was lacking God's perspective and as a result, locked them into an ungodly judgment.

Another Solution

It is important to recognize that when you confront an area of disagreement you are looking for the possibility of a positive outcome.

Confrontation always involves differing opinions. When no sin is involved, you must approach it from the perspective that each of you may have a part of the solution and that God is waiting for your mindsets towards the issue or one another to change. Then He can release His wisdom and purposes into the situation.

Godly relationships have built in them the requirement to confront for the sake of another. This is particularly so when you behave in a way that is irresponsible or where you take others for granted through dishonor, neglect or sin. These attitudes need to be challenged in a way that confronts the sin, but doesn't bring judgment onto the person.

It's not an easy thing to do, because we do not see confrontation as a gift. We are not naturally good at it. However, you must learn to do it. For the majority of people, the notion that you must confront to help yourselves and others grow is a foreign idea. The inherent problem with addressing people's issues is that they don't always want to resolve them, and their responses may not always be godly.

If someone cares about you, but is afraid to talk to you about a difficulty you are having or causing, then *their fear of your reaction is greater than their fear of God*, since they are willing to leave you in that place of irresponsibility, ignorance or sin. Rather than face the possibility of your displeasure, anger or even your withdrawing from their lives, they are willing to abandon you to your error or sin. *"Again, when a righteous man turns away from his righteousness and commits iniquity, and I place an obstacle before him, he will die; since you have not warned him, he shall die in his sin, and his righteous deeds which he has done shall not be remembered; but his blood I will require at your hand. "However, if you have warned the righteous man that the righteous should not sin and he does not sin, he shall surely live because he took warning; and you have delivered yourself."* Ezekiel 3:20-21

If you are in relationship with someone who suddenly becomes cold or cuts you off, you can conclude that there has been an offense somewhere, but if they refuse to address the issue, there's not much you can do about it. When you become aware of the strain you need to confront. How you confront is significant. "I don't know what happened, but I sense a tension between us," or "I would like this relationship to come back to a good place and I am willing do whatever it takes." "I'm feeling like something has happened between us. Is it something I said or did? Can we talk about it?"

When you don't confront, you compromise. Believing that you are being tolerant, you fail to bring clarification or correction where it is needed. *"Brethren, even if anyone is caught in any trespass, you who are spiritual, restore such a one in a spirit of gentleness; each one looking to yourself, so that you too will not be tempted. Bear one another's burdens, and thereby fulfill the law of Christ."* Galatians 6:1-2

The problem with not confronting is that you learn to disregard the small problems and sweep them under the carpet until they become a stumbling block or there is an emotional explosion.

As stated before, confrontation doesn't have to be an adversarial event. It is a way of clarifying confusion and dealing with pain; "I'm getting the impression there's something wrong." "Is there something wrong? Is it something that I've done or am I misinterpreting what's going on?" By presenting the issue in a way that places the onus on yourself, it becomes more acceptable and easier to address.

"I'm getting this impression that something is not quite right and I may be wrong; would you help me clarify it?"

"Help me see if I understood this properly."

"I think I am hearing you say…"

However we phrase it, we do it to bring clarity.

If the other person is afraid to tell you what's on their mind, (because of their fear of rejection, anger, hurting the other, or of authority figures), then at least it's out in the open. Then pray. "Lord I've taken offense, please forgive me," or, "Lord, this hurts. I forgive them; please help me work through the pain."

You are going to face these situations. They are prevalent in so many relationships. Paul says, *"If possible, so far as it depends on you, be at peace with all men."* Romans 12:18 Make every effort to be at peace, but if that isn't accomplished, you have done what you needed to do. Then leave it alone. You can't always bring restoration. Sometimes you need to give the Lord time to bring healing into the situation and the people involved. However, you can always ask the Lord to bless them or you can intercede for those you have offended or who offended you.

Judgment and Compromise

By failing to confront the problem, you are condoning an action that is contrary to the heart and will of God. By not living up to the standards you proclaim, you may be creating an offense and a scandal in the eyes of those who observe the situation.

This becomes an even greater concern if you are in a position of leadership, since you are now modeling that it is acceptable to submit to a wrong behavior or way of thinking.

Keep in mind that you must make a stand for what is righteous, realizing that:

There is a difference between observation and judgment.

There is a difference between disagreement and judgment.

There is a difference between confrontation and judgment.

Lawlessness

If you don't confront issues, you can easily encourage lawlessness.

An extreme example: if somebody steals something from you, he breaks the law. You must respond by taking some action to bring resolution, whether you confront the person or call the law. If you don't do anything, you wrap yourself in the mantle of a victim and enable someone to become a lawbreaker.

However, whatever action you take, it must come with it a large amount of grace and the expectation of redemption. You must ask yourself, "What can I bring into this event that gives glory to God?" You may have to ask Him to show you His heart for this person. Your approach needs to be redemptive. "Lord, how do we bring your presence into this situation?"

Simply forgiving the other person and letting the issue drop enables lawlessness, keeping them from growing in responsibility and wholeness. As hard as forgiving can be, it is harder yet to hold that person accountable without condemning them. That is the difficult thing that must be done for the sake of all involved.

You don't judge, but you also do not enable lawlessness. When Jesus says turn the other cheek, I don't believe that He tells me to be a victim. He simply says, don't react and take justice into your own hands. Let the need for personal justice never be greater than your desire for healing and righteousness in the perpetrator.

What You Value You Protect

Your willingness to confront is usually determined by the value you attach to the issue at hand, whether they are people, beliefs or things in your life. Those things you value most you are willing to work through and fight for, which usually means there will be a certain level of confrontation.

However, there are other things in your life that are really not that significant. You can accommodate one another without them becoming points of contention since in the long run they really don't matter.

Most of you find that the way you approached confrontation in the past hasn't really worked. Yet, you persist in doing it the old way simply because it's familiar or the only way you know how to do it. Unless you change the way you confront, you will continue to behave the same old way with the same results.

It is for your good and for the good of others that you must change the way you resolve differences; "We are going to confront this issue. However, we are going to do it differently." You must ask for God's wisdom when you do so.

There is an example of judgment in Acts 2 when the disciples, filled with the Holy Spirit, stumble out into the streets of Jerusalem. There had been the sound of a violent wind in the upper room and now the street outside the house is filled with people who recognized that something unique was taking place; not only that, but the disciples of Jesus, these men from Galilee, are speaking in different languages. Something strange was happening.

However, when the people began to witness the working of Holy Spirit, something else also happened. A judgment was passed by way of explanation. "These men are drunk!"

Peter immediately confronts the challenge. He doesn't say, "You are wrong. This is God!" He simply says, "It's not as you supposed. Let me explain what is happening here." He confronts, but it is not from an adversarial position. He wants to clarify what is happening, rather than attack those who have judged.

"People, this is not what you think. You don't understand what is going on. I would say, I don't even understand what's going on. However, this is God."

Because he confronts in a godly way, 3000 were people received into the kingdom. What would have happened if he had said nothing for fear of offending? Worse still, had argued with those who were accusing them?

There had to be this confrontation because they were seen and judged as "offensive." They looked drunk, acted drunk; for all practical purposes, they were drunk, and they were Galileans, assumed to be uneducated and rowdy. They were behaving as was expected of them. Yet, something in them was touching the people. God would not allow the detractors to keep His revelation and life from those who were open to Him.

That was the beginning of the city being filled with the Gospel.

If Peter hadn't confronted, we don't know what might have happened.

Later in Acts 4 they are confronted again. *"But Peter and John answered and said to them, 'Whether it is right in the sight of God to give heed to you rather than to God, you be the judge; For we cannot stop speaking about what we have seen and heard.'"*
Acts 4:19-20

Later still, they are arrested and taken to the Sanhedrin. The

Pharisees wanted to kill them. (Acts 5:20-40) One wise teacher says, "We've been here before. So and So came, said he was the Messiah... We just let them be and at the end of it, it came to nothing. Don't condemn them. Let's see what God does with this. If God is in this, you can't stop it." The Sanhedrin listened to his advice but still insisted, "We've been offended and we need some satisfaction. Let's beat them anyway." This is often the ungodly response to offense.

Forgiveness and Accountability (Restitution)

God forgives you, but you are still accountable for your actions. If you rob a bank and you repent, God will forgive you. However, you still need to make restitution. There are always consequences for breaking the law. Forgiveness doesn't excuse you or condone your actions, but it frees you to be back in relationship with Him and others.

> *"If a man steals an ox or a sheep and slaughters it or sells it, he shall pay five oxen for the ox and four sheep for the sheep.* Exodus 22:1

> *Men do not despise a thief if he steals To satisfy himself when he is hungry; But when he is found, he must repay sevenfold; He must give all the substance of his house.* Proverbs 6:30-31

> *"Zaccheus stopped and said to the Lord, 'Behold, Lord, half of my possessions I will give to the poor, and if I have defrauded anyone of anything, I will give back four times as much.'"And Jesus said*

86 | Judgment, Disagreement and Confrontation

to him, 'Today salvation has come to this house, because he, too, is a son of Abraham.'" Luke 19:8-9

In the Christian community restitution is seldom mentioned. It is rarely considered a necessary step to healing. You may be forgiven, but if you don't make restitution, you have not understood the impact of your actions and how they have dishonored and devalued the significance of the other person. There has been a disservice in the body of Christ by failing to emphasize that there are consequences for what you do.

If I borrow one of my Christian neighbors' power tools and damage it, he may forgive me when I give it back, but he still has a broken power tool. Next time I ask to borrow anything, he is in all likelihood not going to trust me with his possessions and rightly so. If I have it repaired, that is better, but the power tool is still not as good as it was. However, if I really value the relationship I will buy him a brand new replacement.

I will say, "I broke your tool you lent me. Will you forgive me? And because I value our relationship so much, I bought this new one for you." I have just come in the spirit of restitution. What I am saying is that the relationship is worth whatever it costs me. A breach of relationships is rarely approached from that perspective.

It is important to understand that there is an absolute need for restitution. If someone loses or damages your possessions or reputation, you have an expectation of restitution. However, if they don't make restitution, you can't judge them; you must let it go. If restitution does come, you acknowledge it: "Thank you for valuing the relationship. I really appreciate that in you."

Judgment Must Have the Expectation of Reconciliation

Jesus tells you to be reconciled, to be brought back together with those from whom you are estranged; that is the heart of God for you.

> *"For if while we were enemies we were reconciled to God through the death of His Son, much more, having been reconciled, we shall be saved by His life. And not only this, but we also exult in God through our Lord Jesus Christ, through whom we have now received the reconciliation."*
> Romans 5:10-11

> *"Therefore if anyone is in Christ, he is a new creature; the old things passed away; behold, new things have come. Now all these things are from God, who reconciled us to Himself through Christ and gave us the ministry of reconciliation, namely, that God was in Christ reconciling the world to Himself, not counting their trespasses against them, and He has committed to us the word of reconciliation. Therefore, we are ambassadors for Christ, as though God were making an appeal through us; we beg you on behalf of Christ, be reconciled to God."* 2 Corinthians 5:17-20

> *"For it was the Father's good pleasure for all the fullness to dwell in Him, and through Him to*

> *reconcile all things to Himself, having made peace through the blood of His cross; through Him, I say, whether things on earth or things in heaven."*
> Colossians 1:19-20

It's the Father's desire that none would be lost. He began the process of reconciliation through Christ Jesus and you are to continue the process. Whether anyone is reconciled or not, is their choice. However, the opportunity for reconciliation must always be there. You cannot make any judgment which does not have at heart the objective of reconciliation; otherwise you create a stumbling block that brings separation.

I used to enjoy the place of making a judgment, wanting to see justice at the cost of mercy and grace. Then one day God asked me, "What makes you think you are so different from those you judge?"

The moment you entertain a condemning judgment about anyone, you open the door for separation and bitterness. You need to lay that judgment at the foot of the cross. It's not an easy thing to do, but it is an absolutely necessary thing to do. At the end of the day, any unforgiveness you are carrying is going to come back on you.

Chapter 7

God's Ownership and Makeover

The apostle Paul says, *"Do you not know that your body is a temple of the Holy Spirit who is in you, whom you have from God, and that you are not your own? For you have been bought with a price: therefore glorify God in your body."* 1 Corinthians 6:19-20

When you come to Jesus, He gets you "as is," as a "fixer-upper," as someone who has gone through the damage that the world and the enemy have inflicted. He wants to transform and restore you to His original design and purpose. *For I am confident of this very thing, that He who began a good work in you will perfect it until the day of Christ Jesus.* Philippians 1:6 He wants to remove all the "worldly stuff" you carry. Everything that does not reflect your intended nature must go.

As you are sanctified, the transformation into new way of living is not always an easy or comfortable experience. You find that you still want to have a say in how your life is shaped, or at least be God's consultant during the process.

You fail to realize that as the previous owner you no longer have a right to say, "I don't want to do this." Or "You can't do that." The new owner simply looks at you and says,

> "The old furniture (ungodly beliefs) has to go."

> "I'm going to take some walls (forms of self-protection) out."

> "The little windows (insecurities) are going to be changed. I'm going to put in big picture windows so that everyone can look in here."

He says, "You no longer own this place; it's Mine. I am going to restore it to its original design and purpose. I want it to be light filled and attractive, a place where people can come to feel and receive life and enjoy themselves."

The natural response again is, "Lord, they may take advantage of me; they could even end up using me!" He however seems very happy about the whole thing. "Yes, but, you are being a vessel thru which My light shines. I am going to change you and make you into a life-giving place for others."

> *"And do not be conformed to this world, but be transformed by the renewing of your mind, so that you may prove what the will of God is, that which is good and acceptable and perfect."*
> Romans 12:2

He wants to change you, to make you different, by molding you to His image, not the world's. For Him to do this, you must be willing to be renewed at the core of your being, so that you effortlessly reflect the character of Christ. This means you must be transformed from the accepted patterns of the world into the patterns of heaven. In Christ, you cannot go back into the old and familiar ways of being. You cannot remain in the "old neighborhood," and you can no longer agree with the ways of the world.

"Be transformed." Literally, be metamorphosed, changed from the inside out so that everything about you is different. That happens in the heart, a hidden place, where you are being changed from glory to glory. *"But we all, with unveiled face, beholding as in a mirror the glory of the Lord, are being transformed into the same image from glory to glory, just as from the Lord, the Spirit."* 2 Corinthians 3:18

It's the work that He does. You only need to agree, submit and allow Him to do it. The new life flowing in and through you will be tested as you learn to relate to others in a way that reflects the life giving nature of Christ in you. Your response to the words and actions of others is a good measure of your growth.

"Lord, where have I been offended today?

"What has that revealed in my spirit about me?"

God's View versus Your View

God wants to deal with those long standing judgments that continually seem to disqualify you, in exchange for a new identity washed by grace and mercy.

In the past, when I looked in the mirror, I did not like who I saw and my reaction was not always godly. There was the usual, immediate judgment and pronouncement, which declared how my day was going to go. 'Oh, man, who do you think you are? How are you going to fake it today?' I did not want to show what I saw to the world, so I offered what I thought would be acceptable, something they would not reject.

It was a constant struggle.

A Life Changing Question

One day God asked me this question, "Do I love junk?"

Somewhat taken aback I said, "No."

The moment I said, "No" I knew it was a setup.

Then He asked, "Do I love you?"

I said, "Yeah... You love everybody."

I was quite comfortable being a part of a mass of people, or in the church, but as an individual it was a different story. I was very uncomfortable with God. He loves all of us; it's a blanket He throws over us. Whether we "deserve it or not," we're all under it. However, when He focuses on me it becomes a different story.

"Do I love you?" He asked again.

Reluctantly I said, "Yeah..."

Then He asked, "What does that make you?"

I recognized that this conversation was going in an uncomfortable direction, where I did not want to go. Finally I acknowledged that since He loves me, "That makes me lovable."

Then He said, "In the mornings, look into the mirror and declare to yourself 'I am lovable.'"

I did it for a while, and then I would forget. My heart was not in it, but He would gently remind me again. I was uncomfortable, but I was being obedient. However, the interesting thing was that the words began to have an impact on me. After a while I would get up in the morning and say, "I'm lovable" and it changed my outlook about myself and my day. His judgment of me made a difference! As I accepted that His love for me made me lovable, it had an effect on me and the people around me. It worked!

Then one day as I was getting ready to teach a class, God spoke to me, "I want you to tell the class that you're lovable." I thought, "I'm smart enough." I will just slip it in as part of the teaching and nobody would be the wiser. However, the Lord continued, "No, I want you to tell them."

I'm saying, "I'll figure it out."

As I'm having this discussion with Him, I am suddenly walking to the front of the room. I wanted to stop, but my legs were not listening to me. As I walked up on the platform, I asked the worship team to stop. I couldn't believe that I was doing this; I could not remember ever feeling this uncomfortable.

I say to the class, "I have something…very important to say."

They listen attentively. "I need to tell you that…I'm extremely lovable."

There was total silence. Nobody laughed, which is what I expected; they somehow knew this was a God moment.

Then I turned to the worship team and asked them to continue.

As I walked to the back of the room I was thinking, "I can't believe what I just did." Now the enemy is telling me, "Man, you're egotistical, self-centered and you sure made a fool out of yourself."

All I could say was, "It wasn't my idea."

I needed to make a public declaration of what God had been telling me in private: to break out of my isolated world, where I was only in a halfhearted agreement with how God saw me. Since I still didn't fully believe His word enough to have the courage to declare the truth about how He saw me, I was pushed into breaking the standoff by declaring publicly what He had been telling me in private.

I had doubted His word and His heart for me, and so I lived in the ambivalence of, "God says this…but I know different…" I was still operating under a personal judgment of failure and rejection, a judgment that declared no one would truly love me, and those who did would probably leave sooner than later.

The declaration of those negative judgments created in me the beliefs that became my identity. These judgments were so powerful that for the first 10-15 years of my marriage, I fully believed that when my wife came to her senses she was going to leave me. Since I could not love myself, how could she possibly love me? How could she possibly find anything of value in me when I couldn't?

Most of you have lived in those places where you feel disqualified through the judgments you or others have made about you. The sad thing is that when you embrace the judgment, it becomes part of who you are.

You are only a failure if you embrace failure and use it to condemn and label yourself, making it part of your identity. As you continue to condemn yourself, you create the labels that will lock you into "failure," "hopelessness," "insecurity" and so on. Because you accept and therefore believe the judgments, they now become part of your identity. You condemn yourself to live with the labels such as: "I am a Failure." "I am Unlovable."

Now for the sake of the labels you believe to be true, you must sabotage anything you do that opposes that identity, because there is no room for success in the identity of "Failure." These labels determine your reactions to events in your life and to the things you do. When you make a mistake, the first thought that crosses your mind is determined by what you have already accepted about yourself.

Is it, "Ah man, how can you be so stupid?' or is it, "Thank You Lord, for another opportunity to learn."

Learning to Learn

As a child, one of the absolutely necessary things needed for growing into a mature healthy adult is the freedom to fail and to learn from your mistakes, to have those experiences of failing explored in a nonjudgmental way.

> "You're smart enough, you can learn from this."

> "Let's explore what happened."

> "How would you do it differently next time?

> "That was painful wasn't it; what could you have done differently?"

This was probably not the experience of most children. Those who mentored us were for the most part impatient, broken people who were never properly mentored themselves, and therefore not equipped to help us grow through the small and big failures we faced as children.

Your early failures, rather than being corrected with life giving instruction often drew criticism and condemnation that you believed to be true. Because you accepted the description of who you were very early in life, you were already being disqualified.

In God's sight you are extremely significant and valuable, but the judgments of others and your acceptance of those judgments have led you to believe and embrace the condemnation that says otherwise, creating in you deep insecurities and uncertainty about who you are, to such an extent that you can't even believe God's truth about you.

God wants you to move from that place to a new place where you can declare and accept His truth about you, which is, that you are extremely significant and valuable in His sight.

> *"When I consider Your heavens, the work of Your fingers, The moon and the stars, which You have ordained; What is man that You take thought of him, And the son of man that You care for him? Yet You have made him a little lower than God, And You crown him with glory and majesty! You make him to rule over the works of Your hands; You have put all things under his feet,"*
> Psalm 8:3-6

As you begin to accept the reality of who you truly are, you will discover that you become less judgmental about yourself and others. Now, anytime you make a mistake you can, you must say "Lord, please forgive me. I am behaving in a manner that is beneath whom you created me to be." God's truth about who you are must permeate the core level of your being, so that when you walk into any place you can truthfully say, 'Thank You, Lord, that today I am going to be a blessing because You're fully alive in me.'

Since you are in Christ and He is in you, He is with you wherever you are. However, your negative judgments about yourself blind you to that truth and, as a result, you fail to manifest Him to the world around you.

God's Attitude versus Your Attitude

Transformation, Judgment and Observation

It is important to recognize and accept that you must be transformed. You may not enjoy the process since it means letting go of some of the things you hold dear. One of the things to give up is the habit of judging others based on your interpretation of what is right and wrong. More often than not, these are the self-righteous judgments that will cause division rather than an opportunity for restoration. When you stop judging, it seems that suddenly you are losing a job you did rather well.

When I am offended, my regular attitude is still one of "Lord, you saw what happened, what are You going to do about this?" I must learn to defer judgment and not demand or even want justice or retribution, but to leave the resolution with God.

One day, His response to my cry for justice was, "Wow, have you seen them?"

"Just wait until you see all the blessing I've got planned for them."

Puzzled, I said, "Wait a minute. You don't seem to understand that your favorite child, me, is not feeling understood right now."

He ignored my comment saying, "I have such plans for them. I'm going to bless them. I'm going to nurture them, grow them. I'm going to do all these wonderful things for them."

Even more puzzled, I said, "What am I, chopped liver?" because I still wanted my pound of flesh.

The lesson He is trying to teach me is that every time I get offended, I need to ask Him how He feels about the one who offended me. I, however, continue to say, "Lord, You don't seem to understand my situation here. I have been hurt, cheated, abused…"

He is saying, "I understand, but I died for them as well!"

He wants you to see others from a heavenly perspective. That does not mean that you play the victim, but rather that your first response is to look for a way to bring redemption into the situation.

"Take Every Thought Captive"

A few years ago, I suddenly began to experience constant headaches. This was unusual, since I seldom got headaches.

People would pray for me, and as they prayed the headache lifted. Soon after however, the headache was back; it would not go away. We couldn't figure it out. We prayed for everything we could think, but it would still not leave. This continued for a few months. Then one day as we were praying, suddenly someone got a revelation about it. As we prayed into it, the headache lifted; it was gone and did not return.

The Lord quickened to me, "There is something I wanted you to learn."

It had to do with my thought life.

He told me, "Any ungodly thought, any condemning judgment that you entertain will give the enemy easy access to you."

"Lord, why didn't you tell me this in the first week?"

His reply was very interesting and very true; He said, "Because you would have forgotten."

It was so critically important for me to understand this, that He allowed the pain to continue until I was sure not to forget it. These were not the overtly sinful thoughts; these were what I considered the "righteous" thoughts and judgments about people and life. Therefore it was something I needed to go through to learn at a greater depth.

Thoughts: Their Source and Consequences

I have not forgotten the event. It doesn't mean that ungodly thoughts don't come my way – but what I do with them is critical.

It also brought a greater understanding and appreciation for what Paul says in 2 Corinthians. You must immediately take your thoughts captive. Be suspicious of them, rather than giving them any time in your mind. Be violent about dealing with them! "*We are destroying speculations and every lofty thing raised up against the knowledge of God, and we are taking every thought captive to the obedience of Christ, and we are ready to punish all disobedience, whenever your obedience is complete.*" 2Corinthians 10:5-6

The words in these two verses are violent: "Destroying," "Taking captive," "Punishing."

The Lord makes it clear, "As long as you allow any of these thoughts to have a foothold in your mind, you are exposed and the enemy will easily target you." You must be intentional when you begin to address the thoughts that so easily ensnare you into that which has no true life or benefit to you or others. These thoughts were subtle, but powerful places of admittance for the enemy. When you entertain negative thoughts to any extent, you become very visible to the enemy. In my case, they were mostly the judgments I had entertained about the people around me: coworkers in the Kingdom, leaders and fellow believers.

Captured Thoughts Create Immunity

Holy Spirit will quicken to you those thoughts which are not life giving. When your thoughts are ungodly in any way you become a well-lit landing pad for the enemy. Therefore, capturing your thoughts gives you a great level of immunity. As long as your thoughts are godly, you are protected from being accessed in ways that are easy for the enemy and destructive for you. The purity of thoughts towards others increases your ability to discern the strategies of the enemy, so that you can more easily recognize what is of the demonic realm and what is of the flesh. This is particularly significant when you are dealing in the area of witchcraft, since it thrives on a rebellious thought life.

God Reveals Where Changes are Needed

Recently, I started having headaches again.

Again I went to the Lord. "Lord, what is this? What do I need to learn now?"

After a short while the headache began to lift and we started getting revelation about what was happening.

The revelation was that as God was using us in a number of areas, people began to recognize and value us and what we did. They were grateful for how the Lord had worked through us to affect their lives.

However, as this happened, I became very uncomfortable and started to minimize what they said about God's work through us.

"That's silly," I thought. "Anyone can do this."

Apparently that was a place where the enemy had access to me. By accepting who I am in Christ, but not acknowledging that "God works through me," I was opening a door for the enemy. I needed to embrace that God has gifted me and as He works through that gift it makes me a blessing in the Kingdom. It doesn't make me better than anyone else, it just makes me unique and different from the other person, who is also unique and different and gifted and needed.

This is an important truth to see and understand.

I had made a judgment about myself that had given the enemy access to harass me on a regular basis. Rather than valuing and delighting in the gift that God had given me, I had devalued it. I was uncomfortable with being noticed as He operated through me. He has been saying to me all along, "Be comfortable with who you are. That's how I created you."

Having people acknowledge what we did was not threatening to God, but only to me. I was afraid of pride, and that fear allowed entrance to a religious spirit of false humility. This also created in me a fear that God was going to be upset with me for feeling good about using the gift he had given me.

Many of you may get to the place where you stop judging other people, but will continually judge yourselves. When you begin to question whether God would really work through and with you, you are questioning His nature. It is a judgment against His character and His purpose for you, and is therefore sinful.

Renewal Equals New Truth and New Walk

You need your mind renewed—to learn what is true and valid and what is not.

Anything that brings separation through condemnation has to be taken to the cross. You have to learn God's truth and the meaning of love.

You must learn to accept that when you walk in truth, it might separate you from others, but that the fear of separation should not keep you from choosing that path.

His love maintains an open door for future restoration. Do all you can to maintain relationship, but if others will not accept who you are, it's wisdom to back away, to move out of the situation so that you don't compromise the life of Christ in you. *Never pay back evil for evil to anyone. Respect what is right in the sight of all men. If possible, so far as it depends on you, be at peace with all men.* Romans 12:17-18

Being Changed Can be Messy!

On this path of transformation you will need the help of others, since the journey can be painful, chaotic and at times confusing. You may prefer a predictable, peaceful quiet life, but that doesn't always happen. In this season of change, God seems to have you in a place where you are constantly moving from one kingdom level to another. As you do so, you are going to experience some failures. You may mourn, resist, and rail at God. At other times you may even be ready to quit.

Yet, He causes all things to work together for your good. It may sound difficult, and it is, but in reality it's the love of God. He has you in a state of transformation, in a process, where He is changing all that you thought was important in your life into what is true and significant. You're moving from darkness into light and from being unfamiliar with the ways of God to becoming familiar with the heart of God.

As you recognize that you are being changed, your old life patterns and thinking will be challenged, since you can no longer conform to the patterns of the world you are in, a world you no longer belong to. *"And do not be conformed to this world, but be transformed by the renewing of your mind, so that you may prove what the will of God is, that which is good and acceptable and perfect."* Romans 12:2

However, your old patterns of thinking are so familiar that they are normal to you. You do not even notice them as they operate in your life. The battle is to take those "normal" thought patterns captive. Therefore, continually ask the Holy Spirit to reveal those obstructive belief structures which thwart your growth. He is asking you to let go of a number of things. One of the key things you must abandon is the habit of judging others.

Never forget: you are called to judge actions not people. As Jesus said, *"Father, forgive them for they do not know what they are doing."* Luke 23:34

You will make mistakes, but through them you're being taken from glory to glory and you're being perfected on a constant basis. As part of this growth and change, you must extend forgiveness and grace to yourself when you make a mistake. It may be a difficult or awkward thing to do, but you must agree with God and forgive and release yourself.

One Another

At the end of His life on earth, Jesus said to His disciples, *"Love one another."*

He left the hardest command to the very last. It doesn't seem instinctive to do so. If you've been married, or in a relationship more than a few days, you know there are some issues that are going to come up. It's not easy to love unconditionally. The only ones who can love unconditionally are those who have become Christ like, who no longer have a sense or a need for self-protection or self-promotion.

A mandate of the New Testament is to get you to a place where you are willing to live "for others." We are told in Scripture that you are to "Do...for one another." This requires a change in the very core of your being.

That sounds good in theory, but can be a problem when you are still in a "for me" mindset. A common response is, "Lord that will work really well as long as 'they' take their part in this seriously." Being reasonably self centered when "others don't do for me" can create resentment or even self-pity that quickly turns into judgments—judgments that can hook you into bitterness and isolation, that separate you from others and block the presence of God from flowing through you.

You Carry Blessings

Begin to look at everyone in your life as vessels needing the blessing of God that you carry. Some people will gladly receive it; others may be offended. When you offend others by who you are, you must be careful not to be offended in turn, being vigilant not to give the enemy an opportunity to bring separation.

God may be telling you, "Ask Me how to pray for this person or this situation."

Bridging the Gap

> "For My thoughts are not your thoughts, Nor are your ways My ways," declares the LORD. For as the heavens are higher than the earth, So are My ways higher than your ways And My thoughts than your thoughts. Isaiah 55:8-9

I always felt that this verse was a statement of separation, when in reality it is a call to change. A caall to become Christ like.

Be imitators of me, just as I also am of Christ. 1Corinthians 11:1

Jesus' thoughts were the Father's thoughts and His ways the Father's ways. You are to think His thoughts!

> "For 'Who has known the mind of the Lord that we may instruct him?' But we have the mind of Christ." 1 Corinthians 2:16

> "And do not be conformed to this world, but be transformed by the renewing of your mind, so that you may prove what the will of God is, that which is good and acceptable and perfect." Romans 12:2

God wants you to bridge that gap. It is not impossible. He built a bridge for you—Jesus. He is stating that as you become increasingly more like Jesus, you will also have His thoughts and move in His ways. When you do, things change.

At the moment, if your ways and thoughts do not seem to be working too well, you will want to know the heart of Jesus. To do that you must have time with Him, reflect on what He said, look at what He did. Embrace His prayers, make them part of your life. They are such a manifestation of the heart of Jesus, reflecting His character and His nature. When you do, there will come a moment when His thoughts become your thoughts, and His ways become your ways.

Chapter 8

Living the New Life
Walking in the Opposite Spirit

How can you bless those you have judged? You just do! It is something you must choose to do.

Your mandate is to live your life with a "For others" objective, so that all you do has the well being of others in mind. As you do this, your life is enriched.

When you're having a difference with someone close to you, particularly your spouse, always come at the issue in a spirit that reflects the heart of Jesus. Before you even begin to deal with the issue at hand, first look at all the ways in which they bless you. Otherwise you will recall old judgments, negative insights and disappointments which can cause even greater conflict.

Look for ways to increase the blessing of this relationship, rather than look for a way to prove the other person wrong. Whatever you face, whether it is condemnation, anger, bitterness or rejection, you are to come in the opposite spirit. This will remove a huge landing place for the enemy in your life.

Look for the Gift

The Lord had to teach me a number of things about the family he placed me in. One of the things I learned was that I needed the experience of living in this family, with all its confusion and prejudices, to bring me to the cross of Christ.

My father was an extremely broken person who gave me 150% of what he had, but he had only about 20% of what I needed. The Lord had to reveal to me that I was focusing on my father's lack rather than the gift. I couldn't be grateful to him for all that he did for me, because I was looking at all the things he didn't do—those things I could judge. I could only see the lack and limitations. There was lack in my life, but there was also a desire on my father's heart to bless.

Was it good enough? Probably not, but that's not the point.

I had judged my father, and as long as I did not release (forgive) him and thank God for him, I held him in a prison of my making which isolated him from me because we could not relate through my judgment.

Neither one of us was free.

He was my prisoner, and I guarded the prison, making sure he did not escape my judgment. Ultimately we were both captives but on separate sides of the wall I created.

I learned that when you declare a general pardon to those you have judged, you can be released from the onerous task of reliving the offense.

"Honor your father and mother as the Lord your God has commanded you, that your days may be prolonged and that it may go well with you in the land which the Lord your God gives you." Deuteronomy 5:16 NAS. My judgment kept me from seeing my father from God's perspective. By breaking the commandment to honor my father, my judgment also alienated me from God. Where I judge I will reap consequences.

Moving Beyond the Offense

It's not that there wasn't some real hurt or harm done in the relationship. Everyone has experienced pain while growing up. However, the expectation has to be that God can do something about it, and turn it into something that brings life, not only to you, but also to others.

In everything that you have gone through, God says, "I can turn all of this around, but it requires your willingness to let go of these offenses." You must let go of the offenses or they can be used to justify your anger, bitterness and the beliefs they form, and as a result you remain unchanged. Through your condemning judgments you create a mindset that keeps you locked into a prison of your own making.

Therefore it is crucial that you take every thought captive examining its contents to make sure that it does not bring more judgments—judgments that will continue to keep you captive. If you do not let go of the judgments, how can you bless those who hurt you? Blessing is a choice we make when we release the offender and intercede for them with God. *"But I tell you*

who hear me: Love your enemies, do good to those who hate you, bless those who curse you, pray for those who mistreat you."
Luke 6:27-28

Your mandate is to live your life "for others." Therefore it becomes all about them.

Some Obstacles that Dim the Light

There are stumbling blocks to look out for, those things which keep you ineffective and your light dull.

>The voice of the people around you.

>Old traditional patterns of thought and doing

>The doctrines of men.

The doctrines of men are those "truths" that you accept and never question, which nonetheless keep you in bondage to a belief that will not stand the test of scripture.

Discouraging words and voices will always have a root in judgment and always create some form of blockage to your spiritual growth.

To navigate these blockages you need to change, to see things from God's perspective. To change requires a different outlook, a new way of thinking or looking at the world around you. You literally must say to your self, "Self, this is not what you suppose it is. You may not understand it; it may not be explainable, but I think the hand of God can change this."

Allow the ways of God to work in you. If it is not of Him, He will show you.

Your Thoughts and Ways must Change

As mentioned earlier, in Isaiah 55:8, God is saying, *"My thoughts are not your thoughts and My ways are not your ways."*

It's not saying, "Look how much better and distant I am." What it says to me is, "Son, you need to change the way you're thinking. You need to change the way you act because I want you to come up here to a higher place. From here you will see and think differently and therefore act differently." When I had that revelation, it gave me such an awareness of the kindness of the Father. "Wow, He's not saying that He's aloof, but He's calling me. He's calling me up and He's drawing me into His place." I needed to look at things differently, from a different perspective, from God's point of view.

God's View of Me (and you and you…)

There is a worship song, "Jesus, Lover of my Soul" with a line that says, "It's all about You, Jesus."

We were in Ireland doing a conference and as we were singing that song, the Lord said, "Yes, you're so right, it's all about Me. However, Martin, from My perspective it's all about you."

I was totally taken aback. That was a whole new thought to me.

He said, "The Garden of Gethsemane was all about you."

"The cross was all about you."

"The shed blood was all about you."

I had not seen this. When I got heaven's perspective all I could say was, "Wow, is that how You feel about me?"

He said, "That's just the beginning."

I had no framework to handle the idea that I was that significant to the Lord.

I just didn't know what to do with it.

I felt overwhelmed.

I kept saying, "Wow! You really mean that? It's all about me?"

He said, "From My perspective it's all about you. Why else do you think I came?"

You truly need to have a heaven perspective of how much you are valued and loved. Once you begin to grasp that, you change. You want to put on the nature of Christ; how can you then not love others? This does not mean that you have to accept or agree with the sinful behavior or the beliefs of others. As you embrace the truth of His incredible love for you, it no longer becomes about how many people you've led to the Lord, but how many have come to the Lord because of whom they see in you. There is no argument against this form of revelation. I want Him to be revealed in and through me in a way that gives life.

"Lord, You do it. Do it. I thank You, Father for Your

goodness, for Your incredible delight in every one of us."

"Teach me to delight in Your delight in me."

"Lord, I have all these barriers that I build that keep me from being a receptacle, a conduit of Your incredible grace, mercy, goodness and love. Help me dismantle them."

Becoming Whom You Behold

You become like those you associate with. You are a reflection of the fellowship you keep. You have to spend time with Jesus, the Light, to become Christlike and let His light shine through you. *For those whom He foreknew, He also predestined to become conformed to the image of His Son, so that He would be the firstborn among many brethren;* Romans 8:29

Learning About is not the Same as Knowing

If I were to study my wife and know all about her and I would be able to show her how much I knew about her, she would not be impressed. She would always prefer that I get to know her personally rather than simply learn about her.

The important thing is to know one another more. Everything else just fades away. Knowing about someone is insignificant compared to being in relationship with them. People are not really interested in what you know; they just want to see how you reflect the one you do know. At the end of the day what you know only impresses me—it doesn't change me—but whom you know makes all the difference.

So hang out with Him. He's very good at making and leaving an impression. *"Now as they observed the confidence of Peter and John and understood that they were uneducated and untrained men, they were amazed, and began to recognize them as having been with Jesus."* Acts 4:13

Grace and Truth

There's this interesting statement in the gospel of John. *For the law was given through Moses; grace and truth came through Jesus Christ.* John 1:17 ESV

The law was given through Moses, but grace and truth came as a person: Jesus. The law, the inflexible rules, came written on tablets of stone, but grace and truth came written on the heart of Jesus.

As you take on the nature of Christ Jesus, you transform the "law" from the rigid external rules and regulations and interpret them through the nature and character of Christ.

> *But God, being rich in mercy, because of his great love with which he loved us, even though we were dead in transgressions, made us alive together with Christ – by grace you are saved! – and he raised us up with him and seated us with him in the heavenly realms in Christ Jesus, to demonstrate in the coming ages the surpassing wealth of his grace in kindness toward us in Christ Jesus.*

> *For by grace you are saved through faith, and this is not from yourselves, it is the gift of God; it is not from works, so that no one can boast.*
> Ephesians 2:4-9 NET
>
> *But "when the kindness of God our Savior and his love for mankind appeared, he saved us not by works of righteousness that we have done but on the basis of his mercy, through the washing of the new birth and the renewing of the Holy Spirit, whom he poured out on us in full measure through Jesus Christ our Savior.*
>
> *And so, since we have been justified by his grace, we become heirs with the confident expectation of eternal life."* Titus 3:4-7 NET

The significance of "grace," (the free unmerited love and favor of God) so essential for bringing truth into a difficult situation, is often forgotten. Truth apart from grace can easily break trust, because apart from grace, truth can become legalistic and judgmental. Because of the very fragile nature of trust, it requires grace to protect it. Grace carries hope; it gives life and it soothes the truth. Grace brings with it an element of trust which changes how truth is received. When truth comes wrapped in grace, the other person is exhilarated by its touch.

We must be aware that truth apart from grace can be very wounding. Christians are to be a people of grace, who present truth in a way that releases life to the one who receives it. Truth without the presence of grace often breaks trust. *"...who*

also made us adequate as servants of a new covenant, not of the letter but of the Spirit; for the letter kills, but the Spirit gives life.
2 Corinthians 3:6

"Lord, help me present this truth in such a way that the person who receives it is edified."

Hard Word

When you must confront someone with truth, ask yourself, "How do I wrap this truth in grace so that it gives life?" That has to be the intention. However, there are times when truth must be presented in such a way that it will shake the hearer.

There was a time when Jesus addressed the Pharisees and the Scribes using some very hard words:

> *"But woe to you, scribes and Pharisees, hypocrites, because you shut off the kingdom of heaven from people; for you do not enter in yourselves, nor do you allow those who are entering to go in."*
> Matthew 23:13

> *"Woe to you, blind guides, who say, 'Whoever swears by the temple, that is nothing; but whoever swears by the gold of the temple is obligated.'*
>
> *"You fools and blind men! Which is more important, the gold or the temple that sanctified the gold?* Matthew 23:16-17

> *"You serpents, you brood of vipers, how will you escape the sentence of hell?"* Matthew 23:33

He needed to be forceful with them, but the harshness was meant to release, shake them, to bring them to their senses and open their hearts to the truth. His love for them was evident. Even as He was being crucified, He was interceding for them with the Father. He never stopped loving them.

Paul deals with the man who is sleeping with his stepmother:

> *"It is actually reported that there is immorality among you, and immorality of such a kind as does not exist even among the Gentiles, that someone has his father's wife. You have become arrogant and have not mourned instead, so that the one who had done this deed would be removed from your midst. For I, on my part, though absent in body but present in spirit, have already judged him who has so committed this, as though I were present. In the name of our Lord Jesus, when you are assembled, and I with you in spirit, with the power of our Lord Jesus, I have decided to deliver such a one to Satan for the destruction of his flesh, so that his spirit may be saved in the day of the Lord Jesus."*
> 1 Corinthians 5:1-5

Here he is literally saying, I don't want to destroy him but I want him to come to a place where he can be saved. How do you see Paul's heart in this situation? It can be seen as being very harsh, but in reality if you look at it carefully, it is about bringing salvation and restoration. He wants to bring life.

Your Position

Your default position with truth is always to let it be wrapped in grace. If you can't do it at that moment, pray, "Lord, teach me how to do it in such a way that it doesn't bring division, because that's not my heart." As much as it is possible and up to you, choose to live in peace with everyone. However, sometimes despite your best efforts, division does come. *"If possible, so far as it depends on you, be at peace with all men."* Romans 12:18 Others make up their minds about how they will respond, and there's not much you can do about that.

Grace Needs Truth

There can be harshness when truth is expressed without grace. However, if you extend grace without truth it is not true grace and it is usually ineffective, enabling the other person to remain unchanged. It is often based on the fear of confrontation and the fear of man.

When you are motivated by fear, your primary aim is not to upset anyone, or do anything that will distress them. Therefore the usual choice is to be "Nice" and avoid any possible conflict. The problem with being "Nice" all the time is that people will never be sure where they stand with you.

The fear of offending people will keep you from doing what is right, from speaking the truth or attempting to bring correction into a sinful or potentially sinful situation. In your desire not to offend, in trying to be "Nice" you can easily compromise your integrity and your testimony. That doesn't mean you have to be uncaring or hurtful; it simply means that when you come with truth, you do so in a spirit of grace.

Truth must come with grace, or there is no power to the grace.

If you consistently apply truth with grace, people will know that what you are going to tell them is the truth, but when you do, they are not going to feel condemned or judged.

That's the mandate for all—being the light that reveals truth, and bringing a warning when there is a danger of going off track.

You need Holy Spirit to guide and help you in the process. The wonderful thing is that if you blow it, and you probably will, you have the incredible gift of forgiveness. You repent, you forgive, you make amends, you dust yourself off. You don't beat yourself up and you don't lose sleep over it.

Simply say, "It's been dealt with, Lord; teach me how to do it better next time." God forgives; He pardons and forgets. *He has not dealt with us according to our sins, Nor rewarded us according to our iniquities. For as high as the heavens are above the earth, So great is His lovingkindness toward those who fear Him. As far as the east is from the west, So far has He removed our transgressions from us.* Psalm 103:10-12

Looking for Models to Follow

The world is desperately looking for those who exhibit the attributes of Christ, people who are life givers. I still look for people to come into my life who reflect the nature of Christ, and I make an effort to spend time with them because their lives are contagious, and they are going to affect me with their Christlike integrity. I watch their actions because I still need to see Christ modeled for me. If I just hang around with people who are very "Nice" and "Sweet" all the time, I'm never going to be challenged to change. Therefore, I look for people who are godly, straightforward, and real.

Do I get it right all the time? Probably not, but that should not stop me.

Moving Into Trust

When your trust in God is growing, you will begin to meet the following criteria:

If you trust Him, you will not question His instructions.

That is a tough one because often the Lord's instructions don't seem to make much sense. What He's saying is, "You can't question My instructions; just simply do it." The more you progress into this walk of obedience, the more Holy Spirit flows through you and there begins to be a spontaneity that takes place in your life that is quite wonderful and very delightful.

If you trust Him, you do not need to understand what He asks you to do.

You don't need to understand His instructions; you only need to be obedient. You live in a culture that demands an explanation or understanding of what you do or are asked to do. God simply asks for obedience. Your obedience is based on trust. Without trust you will question His reasoning.

If you trust Him, you don't need to see the results of what He asks you to do.

Doing something without seeing the results is often difficult if not frustrating. It is normal to track the progress of things - to chart, measure, assess and predict the outcome. God does not do any of these; He rests in who He is.

> *"so is my word that goes out from my mouth: It will not return to me empty, but will accomplish what I desire and achieve the purpose for which I sent it."* Isaiah 55:11 NIV

The timing and outcome are in His hands, and only in His hands.

If you trust Him, you don't have to like what He asks you to do.

When you are asked by the Lord to do something, your obedience is a declaration of trust. Your need to understand is a declaration of doubt. You can ask "How?" but not the "Why?" That questions His integrity. You won't always understand it anyway. He may require you to do something today, which has a seed with a future purpose; ie., He may have a plan for an event to take place 150 years from now.

"You mean, Lord, I have to wait for 150 years?'

"Well, when you get up here, time makes no difference."

Ultimately your obedience is a reflection of your relationship with Him. You will constantly come back to that. Obedience builds a Christlike character in you and renews your mind to receive the revelation and wisdom you need in the world today.

It always begins with you. Paul prayed, *"I keep asking that the God of our Lord Jesus Christ, the Glorious Father, may give you the Spirit of wisdom and revelation so that you may know Him better."* Ephesians 1:17 NIV

The main purpose of revelation is not only to get wisdom, but to become whom you behold. Both are a gift from God. Revelation discloses. It reveals something to you. Wisdom is the godly use of accumulated knowledge based on the holy fear of God. When you get revelation, you suddenly understand that which He reveals to you, and you are changed, transformed.

"Lord, reveal to me Who You truly are so that I may be transformed."

It is critically important to learn to trust Him enough to surrender all of your self-serving and self-protecting tendencies so that you may become more like Him. Then when you face difficult situations the old tendency to revert to self-protective judgments is halted by God's wisdom and arrested by Holy Spirit. *"That the eyes of our understanding might be opened."* Ephesians 1:18

In 1 Corinthians we read that we *"...have the mind of Christ."*

"But he who is spiritual appraises all things, yet he himself is appraised by no one. For WHO HAS KNOWN THE MIND OF THE LORD, THAT HE WILL INSTRUCT HIM? But we have the mind of Christ." 1 Corinthians 2:15-16

Paul is not saying that we might, or that we will, or that we could, but what he says is that we have it. So you are not transitioning from one thought pattern into another one, an old way of being into a new way of being, the old way of thinking into the new way of thinking. It is already present in you! *"Therefore if anyone is in Christ, he is a new creature; the old things passed away; behold, new things have come.*
2 Corinthians 5:17

You must reach up to that place that Isaiah talks about in chapter 55. All that you need has already been given to you. There is nothing you can do to earn the mind of Christ, because it's already in you.

All you must do is allow the transformation, the metamorphosis to take place. It only requires your cooperation. You must let go of that which is not of God, by taking every thought captive that is not Christlike. *"We are destroying speculations and every lofty thing raised up against the knowledge of God, and we are taking every thought captive to the obedience of Christ."* 2 Corinthians 10:5

You must capture every thought and search it for any contaminants that can bring the distractions that so easily keep you from pursuing the will of God in your life.

You need people around you who love you enough to tell you the truth. You need people who will encourage you in the process of renewing your mind, who will challenge your statements about yourself and others, making sure that you stay focused on the transformation. They are absolutely necessary for your well being. If you don't have them, ask the Lord to provide them, to bring them into your life. You need people around you who will challenge your walk when it is not life giving, either to you or others.

As you become more like Him, the transformation causes you to become love.

John writes about it in his epistles.

> "Beloved, let us love one another, for love is from God; and everyone who loves is born of God and knows God. The one who does not love does not know God, for God is love." 1 John 4:7-8

> "Whoever confesses that Jesus is the Son of God, God abides in him, and he in God. We have come to know and have believed the love which God has for us. God is love, and the one who abides in love abides in God, and God abides in him."
> 1 John 4:15-16

Your intention is ultimately to be a life-giver.

There are three major things Jesus tells those who belong to Him to watch for. The **Three Don'ts** you must remember:

- Don't judge,
- Don't scandalize,
- Don't carry offenses.

This is a characteristic of your nature in Christ, and therefore, any part of you that does not conform to His standard you need to change.

You are called to become like Him, to love, and to be a life-giver. It is then that His light will shine with a brightness which draws the lost out of darkness.

At the end of the day the Lord is going to shine; He is going to be victorious, but He wants you to participate in the victory, to be alongside Him in the process of bringing light and life into the world. He wants to transform you, to change you; he wants a metamorphosis to take place in you so that where you used to crawl in the darkness, now you have light and freedom to stand erect, representing the Lord who loves you.

Father, bless each and every person who reads this. That which is not of You Lord, turn into dust, blow it away, however, that which is of you plant it deep, water it with Your Holy Spirit and bring it to life and let each one of us Lord in our own unique wonderful way be a revelation of Christ in the lives of others. In Jesus' Name we pray. Hallelujah. Amen.

Visit us online!

For more information about Rushing Streams Ministries, or to contact us, please visit our website.

www.rushingstreamsministries.org
www.martinfrankenaministries.com

Our bookstore now features audio teachings with online sound clips for you to review.

If you would like to host a teaching session with Martin and Cindy, or to inquire about personal ministry sessions, please contact us through our website.

Another book by Martin Frankena

Prayers of Power - Breaking Through to Wholeness

About Martin Frankena

In a teaching and counseling career spanning more than 30 years, author and teacher Martin Frankena has shared the life-changing power of Christ's redemption with individuals and churches in America, Canada, South America and Europe.

Martin and Cindy

Martin and his wife Cindy founded **Rushing Streams Ministries** to further the Lord's mandate of releasing people into freedom from bondages to experience greater wholeness and fulfillment in life. A major focus of the ministry is healing from generational issues.

Martin holds school of ministry throughout the year and travels extensively to share in churches and conferences. Martin's material, including his "*Encounter*" curriculum, is being implemented in churches and retreats throughout North America.

With a Masters in Pastoral Counseling, and a Doctorate in Ministry, Martin is a certified Pastoral Counselor. He has served on the pastoral staff of the Toronto Airport Christian Fellowship, and as Assistant Director of a major international healing ministry. They currently reside in the Baltimore, MD area, and are the proud parents of three grown children and eight grandchildren.

"Martin and Cindy Frankena are two of the very choice servants of the Lord. They have been uniquely gifted and trained to help bring freedom to those in bondage and to minister in the arena of generational prayer and inner healing. They are not only trained to minister, but are trainers of ministers. Anyone who comes in contact with their ministry will be highly blessed."

—Dr. Paul L Cox, Founder, Aslan's Place, Hasperia CA.